GW00671722

LEADERS WITH A HEART

GLOBAL ENTREPRENEURS CREATING MASSIVE IMPACT

What joy awaits discovery in silence
behind the portals of your mind
no human tounge can tell.
But you must convince yourself;
you must meditate and g create
that environment.
            Paramahansa Yogananda

CONTENTS

INTRODUCTION

From a very early age I've always wanted to help, connect, empower, and inspire others. At the start of 2020 I returned to Canada, leaving Hong Kong, a place I loved and considered my home. I asked myself a powerful question: "What can I do that will allow me to help people, bring together and connect people while inspiring and empowering them to do good so that together we can inspire others to do good as well?" That's when my podcast Leaders With A Heart was born, in October of 2020. Little did I know that this would turn out to be the single most impactful decision of my life so far!

My podcast is a platform to show case heart centered entrepreneurs who are building impactful and cause driven businesses. Businesses with a heart, a purpose, and a mission. Sure, we all need to make money, but let's do so in a way that is meaningful, impactful, and purposeful.

Fast forward to now, 220 episodes and counting. It's been nothing short of life changing and countless blessings. I have the honour of connecting with incredible people from all walks of life, all true experts in their respective industries and sectors, and all having one thing in common: being heart centered and doing good, around them and around the world. In their own unique ways.

It is my utmost honour to call these truly enlightened souls, not only guests on my podcast, but my dear friends. Indeed, having had these wonderful heart to heart conversations with them, we've been able to connect at a much deeper level.

I am honoured to bring some of these stories to you. These are truly empowering, inspiring, impactful, and powerful stories. There are so many other stories that could have easily been in this book but for various reasons didn't, mostly due to timing. However, the good news is that this is only the first volume.

Being impactful and making a positive difference doesn't have to be world changing. In fact, not one single individual can change the world by themselves. However, if each and every single one of us do our part in our own unique way, together and collectively, we can create a massive movement, an unstoppable wave and ripple effect worldwide. This is what changes the energy, frequency, and vibration that creates a better world for all of us. This is what my podcast is about. This is what this book is about.

True authentic Leaders With A Heart, sharing their powerful stories of doing good and making the world a better place in their own unique way.

May these stories inspire you to do good in your own unique, beautiful, and special way, to make the world around you a better place.

Godspeed,

Payman Lorenzo, Toronto, Canada, September 6th, 2022.

DR. IRIS PERKINS

CHANGING LIVES FROM THE INSIDE OUT

*A*s a sixth grader, I was on top of the world! A few more months, and I would officially be in middle school. I thought that I had it all together but didn't know that what I was about to face would significantly change my life!

It was during the fall of the year, and I was extremely excited that I was about to get out of school for the Christmas break. This was one of my favorite times during the school year because of all the fun games that were played.

I was very good at games, specifically the ones that dealt with words. I was especially good at the game, *"How many words can you find in the phrase, Merry Christmas in five minutes?"* Unfortunately, five minutes was four minutes too long for anyone who was competing with me. I was able to find quite a few words because of a system I developed, and it was airtight. So much so that I won every time I played the game.

The day before the last day of class, we were told to ensure that all our work was done so we could start playing the games. That day we had a teacher's assistant that came in to help our teacher and she brought quite a few gifts with her to give away as game prizes and this was even more exciting. We played a few games, and I won a couple of them. Then, finally, the *Merry Christmas* game was announced and boy, was I ready for it!

The game started and I began to work my system, and it was working. Before the five minutes was up, I realized that I had so many words that even I was shocked. The assistant was about to ask how many words each of us had. Most of my classmates were excited about thirty-five and forty words, but I screamed out an ungodly number that doubled theirs. I could hear the awwws and noooos coming from my classmates but that paled in comparison to what I was about to hear.

At that moment, my teacher walked back into the classroom just as the assistant was about to hand out the game prize. My teacher whispered to the assistant, *"Who won?"* Then the assistant responded, *"Iris did."* Then my teacher said, *"She always wins. Let's do something else."* I was devastated and hurt at the same time! I thought to myself, *"why do things always have to stop when it's my turn to win?"* The sad thing is, she didn't even know I heard what she said or how it made a severe dent in my soul; I felt defeated.

For decades, I internalized a rejection complex surrounding this incident and it affected my expectations for a great deal of my adult life. I not only verbalized the rejection of, *"why do all the good things have to stop every time it's my turn to receive"* or *"every time it's my turn to receive something good, the rules change"* but the verbalization worked negatively in concert with thoughts of the age-old injustice that I continued to experience time after time.

It was always a struggle getting a promotion, fitting in with groups, and finding success, because I believed the lie that I told myself all these years; that whenever I'm about to win, somebody is going to change the rules, so why should I expect anything good to happen to me or even for me. I was stuck . . . until the day I realized that I didn't have to be.

Fast forward to the future . . . Strangely enough, I'd always felt the desire to fix things and solve problems for people, but I needed to fix *"me"* first. I was miserable, but I genuinely didn't want others to feel the same way I did. So, I began to look for my purpose and calling in life to help others.

One day, as I was studying a lesson that I was going to teach, on vows, judgments, and forgiveness, out of the blue, the 6th grade incident reemerged in my mind. I was shocked! I had forgotten all about the actual event even though I was reliving it every day through the words that I spoke and the mindset in which it left me; I needed to handle this old offense as it was the bane of my successful existence.

Could it be that I'd finally found a solution to my life-long problem? The answer was, YES! It was called forgiveness and renunciation of the negative words that were associated with the event. Once I remembered that event and the negative words that were attached to it, it was easy to track the areas in my life that rejection had disrupted. No, I couldn't go back in time to correct anything, but I was able to get rid of that old soul wound and cut off the power and the effects that it had over me.

I was finally free from the bondage of rejection that I encountered in the 6th grade! So, I started working on my other soul wounds that I was able to identify from years of receiving offense and cut them off me also. Inner healing can be so freeing and life changing.

Since that eye-opening experience, it has become my passion to help others who suffer not only from rejection issues but from any soul wounds that are discovered *(especially those from childhood)*. The most interesting thing was I didn't have to announce what I did. People just began to come to me for help. This is how Fix My Soul came to be and has been going strong ever since.

I have helped thousands of people heal from the inside out, so they can live guilt-free lives and move in their God-given purpose without fear of the rules changing on them.

CHANGING LIVES BY RELEASING THE PAST

When we are wounded in our souls, those wounds remain until we recognize the cause, renounce the consequences, and release the care that comes along with them. They affect the way we think and communicate with others.

It doesn't matter how young we are, hurt doesn't have an age minimum. If hurt and offense remains in the soul for any period, we will constantly see things through the eyes of our inner pain, and our outcomes will duplicate the equivalent.

This was the case for this next story.

I was hosting a forgiveness session and there was a six-year-old boy who attended this session. Although my largest audience is women, this little boy was sitting in with his mother and listening to everything that I said, word for word. His mother told me that he started crying. I wanted to know why. He told his mother, at the age of two years old, he remembered how his father continually assaulted her through physical abuse and it scared him. Even though the assault was not aimed directly at him, fear took advantage of his little soul. He felt, if his father could assault his mother in this way, that he didn't love her. If his father didn't love his mother, then there was no way that his father could love him either.

I walked him through a remember, renounce and release process and in just a little over a minute, his mother said that he was smiling from ear to ear and felt so much peace within himself. That moment was not only a win for this young lad, but it was also a win for me. I felt his emotional pain and I felt his peace. This was one of the most memorable moments in the history of Fix My Soul. I've carried him in my heart since that day.

Now keep in mind that this was not the outcome for every person that I helped, yet, on various levels, they've all experienced some forms of emotional freedom based on their willingness to change.

This is one of the reasons why I love what I do.

CHANGING LIVES BY EXPANDING MY REACH

Inner healing can come in many forms.

For years, I focused only on uprooting soul wounds of trauma and emotional chaos with much success. Yet, there was another opportunity that I failed to employ . . . helping the masses understand their dreams and visions to identify purpose, build character and other curious attributes about themselves.

I've spent over twenty years studying, dissecting, and interpreting my dreams and the dreams of others with great success. This eventually evolved into group webinars, workshops, and lectures from the biblical perspective. Overall, the results were phenomenal! People were empowered to better understand the messages they received through their dreams. They were able to also identify what and whom their dreams were about, and from where they derived.

One of the ladies in the group was shocked to know that a dream she had wasn't just because she ate a hot dog before she went to bed; but it was a message that God wanted her to understand. She was concerned about the elevation in her blood pressure and was trying to pinpoint the source. That night, she had a dream that would quickly change her life. She dreamed that she was standing in a house, and she saw a ferocious dog growling and foaming at the mouth. Extremely terrified of the animal, she was asphyxiated with fear. Then she woke up.

She realized, from a basic training session, that the message was an answer to her concern. That day, the lady had been involved in a terrible argument with her friend, and she was so angry that she used words that made her so ashamed when she remembered them. Then, she started feeling ill. Here is the basic breakdown of the dream:

House - The Dreamer (anything inside the house refers to the dreamer)

Fear (the dreamer felt afraid)

Ferocious Dog – Friend Who Turned Enemy (the dreamer)

Growling / Foaming at the Mouth – Attack or Fear (personality of the dreamer in this dream)

Feeling Ill – High Blood Pressure (original concern)

In the dream above, the dog represented the lady's attitude during the argument. She was afraid of the dog, because it was growling and foaming at the mouth, which explained her disposition. She could only imagine how her friend felt during that argument.

The message she needed to know was that she has an anger problem that needed correction, and she should apologize to her friend, and work on her anger issues. This was the reason her blood pressure was elevated. This message was an answer to her question. Although, it may not be what she wanted to hear; it was what she needed to hear.

After this dream, the lady apologized to her friend for the angry words she spoke to her. Her blood pressure went down to normal soon after she used the remember, renounce, and release process.

I could go on with story after story of individuals that I have been able to help to combat the demons that keep them up every night. It makes me proud to see how the life-long results that they experience serve as a vehicle of impactful change for their lives.

Many have released fears that had them afraid to step into their destiny, afraid of success, afraid of failure, afraid of fulfilling their calling, and afraid of being rejected. I have enjoyed walking with them through this phase of their internal freedom.

As a sharer of truth, who not only enjoys learning new things, but also sharing the information that I know with anyone; my desire is to be completely empty of information, revelation, and application when I die. I want to leave everything that I have absorbed in this world with those who will appreciate my sacrifice, work ethic and matriculation to have the most impact.

If I'm going to influence the world as a leader, I must lead with my heart.

Everyone that I have helped to heal from the inside out, experienced the compassion of my heart. This is, indeed, the quality of a true leader.

EPISODE 1

DR. IRIS PERKINS

Iris Perkins is the founder of Fix My Soul, LLC, a Soul Coach facilitating inner healing, and a believer in Jesus Christ. She believes that the essence of a person is based on the condition of their soul, thereby helping women of faith to find freedom from the soul wounds of life. As a prolific teacher, Iris operates in dream interpretation, simplifying forgiveness, deliverance and soul wound healing without pills, potions, or physical contact.

Affectionately known as the *Doctor for the Soul*, Iris, is a prophetic voice, impacting the world as a speaker, coach, musician, and a #1 Amazon Best Selling published author of seven books in various genres and a contributor to one other book. She has an earned doctorate in ministry and working towards a Ph.D. in Management-Leadership & Organizational Change to possess balanced knowledge for those in whom she serves.

Iris is a 21st century necessity!

Website: www.fixmysoul.org

DR. JAMIL SAYEGH

LIFE CAN CHANGE IN AN INSTANT

"Tell me, what is it you plan to do with your one wild and precious life?" - Mary Oliver

---

THIS STORY MAY BE THE WAKE-UP CALL YOU DIDN'T KNOW YOU NEEDED.

hen I was 19-years-old and in the sophomore year of my undergraduate degree in New York City, our pre-med group went to Albany to fight to keep funding for the program. The faculty asked me to attend to share my experience of how I had benefited from the program. Planning to leave Friday morning and return Sunday evening, on Wednesday while preparing for my trip, this thought crossed my mind, *"Something's not right. Don't go."* It seemed to come out of nowhere so, as most of us do when we receive a message such as this, I ignored it.

The following day the thought continued, and it became stronger and stronger. By Thursday evening this urge, intuition, gut feeling, whatever you'd like to call it, had become so strong that I finally listened. I sent an email stating something to the effect of, *"I'm sorry I can't make it. Something came up."*

Friday came around, a regular day. Saturday... another regular day. But Sunday morning changed my whole life. Moments after I woke up, my father had a brain aneurysm. Imagine a blood vessel, like a tube, in your brain that balloons outward. If you're fortunate, you have one of the worst headaches of your life, you go to the hospital, they take care of you, and hopefully you get to go home.

My father wasn't as fortunate. His aneurysm ruptured.

He was in a locked room at the time, and I broke the door to get him out. If I wasn't home, he would have died right then and there. We rushed to the hospital where he underwent a four-hour brain surgery. We were told his chance of survival was less than 5% given how severe it was, and if he did survive, he'd very likely never wake up from the coma. As you can imagine, the four hours felt like forty years. After the surgery, we found out it was the worst brain aneurysm the neurosurgeon had ever seen, but miraculously, my father survived.

My family and I entered the hospital's Intensive Care Unit (ICU) to see my father in the most vulnerable position I've ever seen a human being. The hospital staff told us that he was in an extremely critical state, that they weren't sure if he would survive, and that he could die at any moment. To give you some context, my father was 49-years-old, a family-practice physician, and one of the top Elvis impersonators in the world. He toured with Elvis' band, performed sold-out international shows, and created beautiful impact through charitable performances for hospitals. He was known around the world as such a beacon of life, light, and love, and everyone adored him. His energy and presence were immense, yet here he was lying in this hospital bed in a coma.

In that moment I had two primary experiences. The first was a sense of helplessness. It felt like I couldn't do anything. I was being told he could die at any moment, and I felt like I was simply waiting for it to happen. The second was a profound sense of regret. I felt that I had taken my father for granted; that I didn't know him the way that I could have. This really bothered me because it felt like I had bought into *the illusion that I have time.* My thought process had been, *"I'm 19, he's 49; I've got 20, 30, even 50 more years. I don't have to get to know this man right now."* Until that point, my priorities in life were running (I was a track athlete), spending time with my friends, watching movies, and playing video games. I didn't ever think, *"Let me really get to know my dad man to man and soul to soul. Let me see what this guy's all about. Let me see what I can learn from him."* For whatever reason, none of this had been in my awareness. I felt like I'd blown it, and I wasn't going to have that opportunity again.

I was immensely blessed to have three more years with my father before his passing. In those three years, we helped him make an almost full recovery. So much of who I am today was forged through the challenges and adversity of that time. After college, I took several years off to be one of his primary caregivers. For the first eighteen months after his aneurysm, I went to bed every night wondering if that was the last time I would ever see my dad, and I woke up every morning in a bit of a fog wondering if it was all a dream.

This experience taught me the value of every day; the miracle that is right now, this very moment.

Did you know that every day 150,000 people don't wake up? The fact that you're reading this right now means that you weren't one of those people. **It means that you still have the opportunity to create all of your goals and dreams.** In addition, if some, or all, of the people you care about woke up too, then you hit the life jackpot right from the get-go. Your day is already extraordinary; *it's already a miracle.* Yet so many of us think something out of the ordinary has to happen in order for us to feel happy, excited, and grateful. I lived most of my life in this unconscious and unintentional way. I now know with every fiber of my being that:

There are no ordinary moments. The ordinary is the extraordinary.

Imagine you are told you only have one more day to live. Walking around your hometown, you experience the warm sun shining on your skin, a cool breeze on your body, birds singing, a loved one's smile, children laughing, a breathtaking sunrise, the smell of delicious food as you sit down to eat, and anything else you'd like to imagine. Knowing that you will never have these experiences again, would these moments seem mundane? Or would you slow down and take in the miracles all around you? You and I both know the answer. So imagine how wonderful your life could be if you slowed down and savored every moment as if it's the last one? Why? *Because it might be.*

I realized that my father is here now, and he might not be here tomorrow, or even later today. He's here right now, so let me make the most of it. My awareness started to expand as I understood that this also applied to my mother, my sister, myself, and everyone I knew and would ever meet - they could all be gone in the next moment; but they're here now, so make each moment count.

I have a couple of questions for you:

·   In what ways are you taking the people you love for granted?

·   Where are the people who are closest to you not feeling your love?

It's so easy for us to say or think, "*Of course I love that person.*" But are you *being loving?* Think of love as a verb. Are you being the expression of love? Most of the time, the answer is, "*Not as much as I would like.*" My invitation to you is to check in with yourself every day and find ways to embody and express love at deeper levels to yourself and others.

In those three years, I experienced some of my highest highs and lowest lows. On the one hand, my prayers were answered. I spent 10-15 hours per day with my dad. We sang together, played music, went for walks and to physical therapy together. We explored deep conversations, watched movies, and so much more. I really got to know him, and he became one of my best friends. I am truly blessed to have had that experience.

On the other hand, after the aneurysm my father was prone to seizures and short-term memory-loss (at times even long-term memory loss). I remember when, after taking care of him for two to three days in a row, he forgot who I was, and we argued about whether I was his nephew. He had seizures in my arms that lasted between 40 seconds and five minutes. Imagine what it was like to have a 200lb+ man seizing in your arms for five minutes while the phone is across the room, you don't have any medical knowledge, and you don't know what to do. These moments were terrifying. It felt like my family and I experienced his death hundreds of times, and yet these experiences made all the other moments, when he and everyone I cared about were alive and well, so much richer and all the more special. Because I never knew when that last moment might be, I did everything I could to bring my love, gratitude, presence, humor, and perspective to each moment. I'm reminded of a Steve Job's quote from a commencement speech he gave at Stanford University, *"If you live every day like it's your last, one day you will surely be right."*

My father passed away shortly after his 52nd birthday. His wake was five hours in duration, and over 7,000 people attended. I shook every single person's hand, and nearly everyone said, *"Your dad saved my life."* It was so beautiful to see people from all walks of life: different cultures, religions, race, dress, everything, and every one of them had the same reason for being there. They wanted to pay their respects to a man they cared deeply about, who made them feel seen, loved, and heard. I was immensely humbled to see the impact he had, and I experienced a profound realization:

Up until that point in my life, I had been playing small. I cared way too much about what other people thought about me. I was afraid of rejection, and because of that, I was robbing the world of my light.

One of my favorite words is *"enthusiasm,"* which comes from the Greek word *"en-theos,"* meaning *"the God within."* When you radiate enthusiastically, you're shining that light, that divine spark, that uniqueness that is you, into the world. What most of us do, however, and what I was doing for most of my life, is wear a mask that says, *"Who do I need to be for you to love me? Who do I need to be in order to be normal, special, validated, popular, part of the group, etc.?"* We wear that mask trying to perform for approval and validation. The key is this:

Even when you do that and think you won that game, you lose.

This is because you never get your own approval and validation. You always have this knowing in the back of your mind that, *"Something's not right; something feels off with who I'm being and what I'm doing."* In addition, all those people who you believe love you - they don't actually know you. They know your mask, who you've been pretending to be; deep down, you already know this.

So, there I was at my father's wake where, as a result of this epiphany, I made a promise to myself, *never again will I rob the world of who I could be.*

I will live from love, not fear. In doing so, I have found that creating a meaningful difference for so many people when I shine bright is not only what I'm here to do, but my experience of life is so much better and more enjoyable when I let who I truly am out to play. Have you also found that your experience of life is so much richer when you're being your authentic self?

In the three years that I took care of my dad, two of my cousins passed away; one was 20-years-old, the other 21. If you asked either of these men when they were 18 what they envisioned for their life, I promise you neither guy would have said they'd be dead in two to three years. *The problem is that we think we have time, and as a result, we live our life procrastinating on our dreams.* We consistently say, "*I'll do it tomorrow.*" What I've seen, over and over again, is that most of the time, tomorrow never comes. This is because when tomorrow comes, you call it today, and then you say, "*I'll do it tomorrow*" once again. Think of it like this:

Today is the tomorrow you said you'd begin yesterday.

My sincere prayer is that you have several more decades to live, to experience, and to love. Consider the following question, "*How much time do I have left?*" Every one of us has the same answer to that question, "*I don't know.*" And yet, far too often we act as if we're never going to die, we play smaller than we're capable of, we allow fear to run our life, and we buy into stories of limitation about ourselves that aren't true. All these create the likelihood of immense regret; but the good news is that it doesn't have to be this way. Remember:

The future is created by what you decide to do right now. You can start to shift how you're living, how you're showing up, and the actions you take today.

Ask yourself:

- Where is my life not what I want it to be?

· What would I love to create and experience instead?

· What's the one action, the one step, I can take now to move my life forward in my desired direction?

As Dr. Martin Luther King Jr said, "*Take the first step in faith. You don't have to see the whole staircase. Just take the first step.*" So often we want to see the whole staircase before we even begin. We want to have certainty about the entire journey before we allow ourselves to take the first step. That's not how life works. What you can see from where you are is your next step. When that next step feels expansive, exciting, interesting, and when it seems like your intuition is pulling you forward, **take the leap**! If some hesitation or fear is present as well, all the better.

When you expand beyond your comfort zone, things may feel unfamiliar. Unfamiliar isn't bad, it's simply not what you're used to. Like everything and everyone else in your life, it will be unfamiliar until it isn't.

Keep going.

Ultimately it comes down to this - *what is calling to you is calling to you for a reason*. Pay attention and explore it. Once you take that step, the next step reveals itself. If you reflect on your life experience thus far, I'm sure you'll see this has been true for you all along. Follow your heart, passion, and excitement to create the impact you know you're here to make. And if you aren't sure what to do, ask yourself, "*What would my future-self thank me for?*" "*Since my future-self is created by what I do right now, which choice leads me closer to where, and who, I want to be?*" Do that consistently, and the rest of your life will take care of itself.

I trust that this story served as a wake-up call for you, and I hope that you take this opportunity to make your life a masterpiece. If I can further support you on your journey, here's what that looks like:

Life doesn't give you what you want, it gives you who you are being. When we work on that, everything changes.

This is the place to come when you are ready to transform your life. Our work together will be intense as I challenge you to look differently at yourself and your life. I am more committed to your evolution than to your comfort. You will never meet someone more committed to your journey than me.

We will release the hidden blocks that have been keeping you stuck, so you can create the health, relationships, business success, spiritual peace, happiness, and fulfillment that you're looking for.

You will wake up from the dream of limitation you have been living in, and return home, here and now, as the fullest expression of yourself. You will become alive again.

Transforming your life, having love, passion, connection, and excitement in your relationships, experiencing lasting happiness, peace, and fulfillment, making your dreams come true, and becoming the version of yourself that you have always wanted to be - these are the best things you could possibly spend your money on. Nothing else you buy will ever come close.

If you are committed to mastery, if you are committed to your own success, and you are ready to take your life to the next level, then let's have a conversation to discover what is possible. Most people's favorite day to change their life is tomorrow; that's why they stay stuck. You can be different. Your life changes when you do.

Now Is The Time!

It has been my privilege to serve you.

Create a meaningful life!

All my love,

Dr. Jamil Sayegh N.M.D.

EPISODE 20

DR. JAMIL SAYEGH

Dr. Jamil Sayegh is an international life, business, and relationship coach, integrative naturopathic physician, energy-healer, master NLP practitioner, the host of the 'Transformation Starts Today' podcast, and the author of *20 Steps to Your Next Breakthrough*. He works with leaders, champions, and high-performers from all walks of life including world-champion athletes, best-selling authors, entrepreneurs, business professionals, and more to experience more peace, happiness, and fulfillment, and create an extraordinary life without regret.

To learn more and to see if or how Dr. Sayegh may be able to support you, visit him at:

Website: https://jamilsayegh.com

DANIEL TIMOTHY CALEB

THE TRANSFIGURED CREATOR

What would a Heavenly world look like on Earth? And, more importantly, how would you imagine expressing yourself in that perfect world? Wouldn't we dress with grace, expressing our individuality? Wouldn't the movies we watch "tel-a-vision"? Wouldn't playing sports simply be an expression of our passion and desire to have fun together? Wouldn't the music we play and listen to be joyful? When we write books or letters to each other, wouldn't we tell all the stories about the richness that life has in store for us? Nowadays, such an ideal world seems to be far away, yet could it really be further than the planet Mars that humanity is sincerely trying to reach?

We will look at the answer to this question later. But my point simply is - if people want to believe in something, they will go out of their way, take a space shuttle if necessary and make it happen, even without the certainty that it might ever happen. No one has ever been there, no one has ever done that. Yet the course is set.

Whether we want to reach the light of stars some lightyears away in a foreign galaxy, or reach for the light hidden somewhere within us to finally reach the stars, it takes the same belief. So where should we go from here?

At least for myself personally, I have always been fascinated by the universe, the stars, the constellations, the galaxies, and the idea of becoming an astronaut one day. But, after assessing my situation critically, I figured that reaching for the stars within me would probably be the simpler option. So, I set myself on the path to live my dream to reach the stars one day, from where I could inspire people to go on the journey to their dreams hidden inside of them. As much easier as this way of reaching the stars might seem, I had to learn the hard way that taking an actual space shuttle to reach Mars might have actually been easier.

Being passionate about artistic and creative expressions since early childhood, I always dreamt of becoming a professional football (soccer) player. I was simply in love with the Arts & Entertainment industry. The many sounds, the colors, the bells and the whistles, the writings and plays and you name it. Nevertheless, little did I know that to make an impact in the creative spheres of Arts and Entertainment, my destiny would be slammed several times in front of my nose. Like an actor taking on different roles, I was forced to reinvent myself from a blank screenplay. This chapter is my life's story about how I bring transformation to the status quo. This is my transfiguration journey; a glimpse into how you can rebirth, restore, renovate, renew, and reinvent yourself wholly.

MY FOOTBALL (SOCCER) CAREER

As far back as I can remember, my heart's desire was to express my natural gifts and talents rather than have a "9-5" job in an office. At the time I wanted to become a professional football player. The platform and fame that comes along with it, was meant to inspire people to follow their dreams as well. However, the education system I found myself in, wouldn't quite agree with a purpose-driven approach. I was told to *"stick to my roots"* as they tried to talk me into an apprenticeship as an electrician.

I know I decided to be on a journey to the star "light", but I hadn't necessarily envisioned myself screwing in light bulbs! Yet, when I got a contract as a professional football player in Italy at the age of 17, that was a lightful moment indeed! I successfully followed my dream of being a professional football player in Italy, Milan, and the UK, London. But, right before my first major international competition, an inflicted knee injury destroyed my career at its genesis. And with this also my hopes of being a famous football player for the sake of inspiring people to discover their gifts and live their dreams.

When I talk about an *"inflicted"* knee injury, I make full use of its meaning. I was a 17-year-old black kid away from home for the first time, in a country I have never been to, not speaking its language nor knowing its culture. Being a pro-football player (and the youngest in the squad) the age barriers didn't exist anymore which exposed me to team colleagues double my age! The economic situation also wasn't the best and to be paid, you had to stand out by scoring goals. I was one of four strikers on our team, yet only two could play at a time. If you have too many horses running the same race, in survival mode the easiest option is to take one out. End of story. Literally!

FASHION MODEL

Even during my time as a pro football player, I was able to have my light-moments in the middle of dark times. I might not have been given the opportunity to light a stadium, let alone to light the global stage, but at least I was able to screw in a lightbulb here and there, giving me hope. Maybe I was meant to be an electrician? NO! (haha!) Part of my good times in Italy was definitely *"La Dolce Vita"* which led me into the Fashion industry.

My pivotal moment of the tragic end of my pro football career, as hurtful as it was, allowed me to explore the hidden creative potential lying inside me. There was simply some light needed to see it. You see? So, I became a fashion model and simply loved it! All the brands, colors, fabrics, drama, scenery and you name it. As I took on different projects and worked with different people, I quickly realized that the deeper realities of this colorful surface weren't reflecting down there anymore. Well, after all, scientists do say that all colors come from black.

Anyways. I was sadly witnessing how the majority of the people were deeply stressed, angry, sad, enslaved, depressed, cunning, and indifferent in this industry. While observing this reality, I realized that it wasn't primarily the people who generated these outcomes, but a systematically cultivated culture and environment. Soon enough, I would also face this "culture" that didn't align with my values and principles. Despite the offered glory and the fame platform I sought to finally inspire people to live their dreams, deep inside me I knew this wasn't the right way. I had no choice, but to step out of the fashion industry to pursue and serve a higher purpose.

THE DISTORTIVE STATE OF CREATIVE ARTS IN THE WORLD

These two major life experiences as a pro football player and fashion model weren't the only ones I encountered. On a smaller scale, I was also present in the music industry and as a poet. Whereas my identity as an actor doesn't seem to have ever ceased. In each of these activities, I encountered the same situations, the same state of beings within people, which ultimately led to the same results. After leaving the fashion industry behind, I took the time to sit back and reflect on the many things I had observed, which stirred this question within.

"What is happening in the Creative Arts World?"

In the quest to find an answer, I have studied the Arts and Entertainment industry as a whole. I intentionally talked to friends and former colleagues I had worked with or who had experience in this space. I listened to their stories and to what they were going through. I read stories about celebrities and successful people I didn't personally know. By the time I was able to gather this information and look at it from a birds-eye view, I could recognize the patterns. Patterns that went beyond those I initially perceived.

My conclusion was that the Creative Arts World is distorted. If the word *"distorted"* is looked up in the Merriam Webster dictionary, they suggest a definition stating, *"something that is altered from its true, natural or normal state, shape or condition"*. The Cambridge English dictionary defines *"distorted"* as something that is *"pulled into a strange or unnatural shape"* or *"changed, especially in a way that makes something worse than before"*. I get goosebumps when reading these definitions, as I can fully relate to them!

Whereas certain misfits of the Creative Arts World might be perceivable from the media, it is much worse on a personal level. There are dark stories hidden inside of creatives that quill out of them as soon as they have left the stage of light. Stories meant to remain behind the scenes. If a distortion is the consequence of something that has fallen from its original state to the worse, what then is the original state and purpose of creative arts? For me it's clear - to celebrate! Making life a celebration, lifting up spirits and moods, creating platforms of people coming together around events to enjoy life to the utmost. Not to merely exist but to live and turn life into a celebration!

THE SOURCE OF INSPIRATION

You might be thinking of this described celebrative lifestyle as a utopia. A thing too good to be true. Remember when I asked you in the very beginning *"What would a Heavenly World look like on Earth?"* Well, celebration is not too far away from it. You may ask at this point what the solution to this celebrative lifestyle might be? An example that can serve to illustrate my point is the music industry. Oftentimes music brings a beat that carries an atmosphere of stress, anger, sadness, or vanity onto us. Through their lyrics, sounds, and energy also comes across a state of mind, a state of heart, a culture and, ultimately, a lifestyle. But, is it a beneficial one?

All music has an origin, a creator. Whereas one might think that the produced music is detached from its producer, this is not the case. In this case, while the message matters, the messenger matters even more! When a creative goes through a rough time, of whatever nature, be it a break-up from a toxic relationship, a fight with a friend that has become an enemy, undisciplined living consuming more of whatever sets your mind on timeout, and you name it, it will affect the art that they create. Study song titles and the mysteries will be revealed to you.

So then, the question to ponder upon then is, "*What is the Source of Inspiration of a creative?*" The Source of Inspiration will determine the resource of the inspiration. The state of being of the artist while creating will determine the state of the art that came out of them. Heartbreak songs remind you of your own heartbreaks, right? Hardship songs remind you of your own hardships... hello? Nothing is higher than its Source of Inspiration. Artists cannot surpass their Source of Inspiration. We need to make the conscious choice to connect to what we want to attract.

To conclude, the answer to the initial question of what's the solution to achieve this celebrative lifestyle? I believe it is, "*to have a Source of Inspiration that carries celebration within*".

The follow-up question then becomes "*How do we get to a Source of Inspiration that carries celebration within it?*" Based on what we have seen so far, the answer would be "*by having an Artist who is celebrating.*"

And so, the ultimate question then becomes *"How does an artist get into a state of celebration?"*

The answer to this question is universal. It transcends the music industry. It goes beyond the Art and Entertainment industry. Rather, it touches the very creative process of every single human being on earth or space.

CEO AND FOUNDER OF "DANIEL CALEB CREATIONS"

Anyways. I haven't finished sharing the end of my story with you yet! I mean the story has no end yet as we didn't finish yet as we just got started yet, but you get what I mean. So, when my career as a fashion model also came to an end, I was once more faced with a blank screenplay on which my former role that I had seen as my purpose also had been erased. I thought to myself that being an actor was cool but I knew from experience that if the director had other plans, my role might be changed or canceled altogether, which I knew too well by experience. So, with the wisdom gained, I promoted myself to director.

This time, in this new executive role, I was able to take up the pen of life to reinvent myself, to fill the white pages in front of me and write a story I could be proud of. A story with meaning, mystery, full of lessons. A story that would inspire, a story that would give hope. This new awareness of being the co-creator of my life opened the possibility to create something to which I could bring the values, principles, and meaningfulness that I could not find in the Creative Arts World. A creation through which I could finally inspire people to live their dreams.

Today, I am the Founder, CEO, and Creative Director of the Luxury Fashion Brand *Daniel Caleb Creations* which creates "*Heavenly Fashion*". It aims to inspire people from all walks of life to rise above the status quo by simply daring to live their dreams, being transformed into their best version, and having fun while changing the world. The *Daniel Caleb Creations' Heavenly Designs* are celebrated for being transfigurative, luxurious, colorful, bold, artisanal, and timeless. While our creations are *"Made In Heaven"*, we rely on the generational *"savoir faire"* of Italian luxury craftsmanship to transform the heavenly creations into earthly manifestations.

Our flagship collection named *"Romans 12:2"* has been inspired by the quote from first century philosopher, Paul of Tarsus, when he wrote a letter to his students in Rome, saying,

"Do not conform to the pattern of this world but be transformed by the renewing of your mind. Then you will be able to test and approve the best outcome for your life." (paraphrased)

In this quote we are all challenged to not live according to conventional wisdom but, rather, to challenge the status quo by renewing our mind in order for us to be transformed and finally be able to live our purpose. Through the seven color stripes of our trademark, each color represents a Heavenly Virtue, which will help you walk to your desired universal success. Our source of inspiration is our seven heavenly values: peace, love, joy, power, life, wisdom, and mercy.

It goes without saying that living the dreams and visions we have in our hearts comes with serious obstacles hindering us to reach our full human potential. Heaven and hell need to be shaken.

Obstacles can come in the form of serpents which symbolize toxic people bringing negativity, skulls symbolizing dead environments not promoting fruitfulness, or even in the form of dragons symbolizing imaginary giants like the limiting beliefs we so often hold in our minds. Overcoming all these obstacles on our journey to manifest our dreams is directly linked to the degree of our personal transformation. Only our transformed self is able to fully live our dreams. With our feet well-equipped, we can spread this Good News. The Universe is the limit.

THE 3 SECRETS OF THE HEAVENLY LIFESTYLE

If you think back to the question I asked you at the genesis *"What would a Heavenly world look like on Earth?"*, do you think that possibility has become more reachable? Could you envision yourself more clearly living in such a Heavenly world? I hope that's the case by now! A society is driven by its lifestyle, a lifestyle is driven by its culture, and the culture will determine the pattern of a world. The key to create a "Heavenly world" is therefore to have a Heavenly lifestyle that is shaped by a Heavenly culture. There are three simple keys to make Heaven on Earth a reality.

The first key to experiencing a Heavenly lifestyle is expressing a Heavenly light, which is synonymous with expressing your natural gifts and talent as a love service to your fellow human beings. This will make you shine bright.

The second key to experiencing a Heavenly lifestyle is embracing a renewed identity, which is synonymous with becoming your greatest version and sharing yourself as a gift to the world.

The third key to experiencing a Heavenly lifestyle is transforming creation, which is synonymous with refining your natural gifts and yourself to the extent to have a global influence and create a legacy that goes beyond yourself.

THE TRANSFIGURED CREATOR

There is one question I have raised without yet answering, *"How does an artist get into a state of permanent celebration?"* The key lies in the personal transfiguration of the artist. The creations of an artist are as healthy and heavenly, or not, as the degree of personal transformation during the creative process. Transformation is like the authority ensuring that all creative processes carry a positive impact in society once they are released from an artist's mind.

I am not limiting this only to 'creatives'. Every human being is a creator. We are the creators, the artists, and the designers of our own lives. With every thought that we think and express, and with every act that we do, we create. Either for the better or for the worse. For the go(o)d or the evil. Thus, the greatest creation we can give light to in our lifetime is the manifestation of our dreams, where we take what was invisible to the visible. You can do it, as I have. The Universe will conspire to make it happen with you, if you only resolve to live your dreams.

Heavenly Greetings To all the Universal Dreamers!

EPISODE 23

DANIEL TIMOTHY CALEB

Daniel Caleb has been passionate about creative Arts & Entertainment since early childhood and successfully followed his dream of being a professional athlete. Before his first major international competition, an inflicted knee injury destroyed his hopes of inspiring people to discover their gifts and live their dreams.

This moment of desperation led Caleb to explore his other creative veins, such as fashion, where he worked with renowned brands as a fashion model. Despite the offered glory, Caleb could not align his own values with those of the fashion industry and therefore refused to pursue further projects that did not serve a higher purpose.

Today, Daniel Caleb is the Founder, CEO & Creative Director of "Daniel Caleb Creations" which creates "Heavenly Fashion". It aims to inspire people from all walks of life to rise above the status quo by simply daring to live their dreams, being transformed into their best version and having fun while changing the world.

Website: https://eu.danielcalebcreations.com

MARY GOODEN

I AM OPEN TO RECEIVE ALL THAT THE UNIVERSE HAS FOR ME

I must have recited this mantra over one-hundred times before I fully recognized its power.

I had been playing small. I was shining in my authenticity, delivering my message and walking my talk on a really small platform. A platform that I created. I danced around the vibration of expansion in fear. Fear that I would lose, that I wasn't enough and that my message didn't carry the power of lasting change.

Sound familiar?

The universe is waiting for You!

Not the idea of you, or the you that you were taught to be.

Not the complicated version that makes everyone except for you happy.

Not the pre-programmed version that stops you from saying yes to fun, play and uncertainty.

The you that can only be discovered by honoring, accepting, embracing and loving the wholehearted being that you are.

It is a wild ride.

I dare you to do it!

I dare you to recite the mantra with intention!

Knowing that every desire you have ever had will be delivered to you!

Now, all I desire to do, is to share this amazing gift with you!

I have spent the last 22 years learning, practicing, researching, and mastering the art of living wholeheartedly on purpose!

What does it mean to live wholeheartedly?

Living from a place of inner balance and harmony – an alignment of what you think, feel, say and do. Through my committed effort along with the practice of yoga, meditation and reiki energy harmonizing, I have fully embraced wholehearted living and discovered my soul's mission and purpose. I am willing to share my experience, guidance and love to support and serve you in the most sufficient and fulfilling way, so that you too can live wholeheartedly on purpose.

It all starts with a great mantra, a short statement that echoes in your mind, especially when you start to feel a decline in your energy or vibration. The mantra that I hold close to my heart is, "I am open to receive all that the universe has for me." With faith, hope, and love as my superpowers, my journey has encompassed first-hand experience and research on the benefits of yoga, meditation, and reiki energy harmonizing. These modalities have led me to self-trust, authenticity, enlightenment and purpose. I have been guided to share my experience and support you in discovering, living and sharing yours.

Let's take a deeper look at these modalities and how they are used to reshape your inner world, as well as some of my experiences and enlightening moments.

It all started with a yearning for something different. I loved a tough physical work-out, I was a runner, weightlifter, a real cardio junkie. As I write this now it was more than likely the insatiable need to be enough, high-anxiety and coffee that provided me with an endless amount of energy. I was a mother, workaholic and a work-out addict. I managed a fast-paced, highly profitable business and taught several fitness classes a week. I was delighted to share my knowledge, expertise and energy with anyone who was willing to listen and try new things. My friend Stacey came in to work one day super excited to share her discovery of a new yoga studio and I was all ears! I was always eager to try new experiences and was somewhat familiar with the movement of yoga, so I decided to give it a try. It was truly love at first feel, the energy that filled the space was calm, peaceful and compassionate. Almost immediately this space become the most desirable part of my week. On Sunday night I would take the "Sacred Music" class, it was a 90-minute candlelight flow, the perfect way to prepare for the week ahead and the instructor Kasia is a treasure that will live in my heart forever. I mention this class specifically because this is where I first received the calling to become a yoga instructor. I remember it like it was yesterday, as I begin to awaken from savasana, coming back to consciousness, I knew in that moment that I absolutely wanted to make others feel exactly as I felt, pure, content and at peace with all things. The very next day I sought out a yoga teacher training program that felt right and my journey of self-study was about to blossom.

It is true what you have heard, life is a journey not a destination. In fact, the darkest moments and experiences in our life bring us the most profound growth. I am certainly not suggesting that you seek the dark moments, nor I am saying that if you haven't experienced the darkness that you are not growing. Honestly, I wasn't exposed to what felt like my darkest moment until 2014, however looking back now It was the brightest experience on my path.

Awakening feels awkward most of the time, an instant where the light breaks through the darkness. It is about getting out of your comfort zone and inviting a positive change in the way you perceive your experiences. What I hope to share with you in the practice of yoga, meditation, and reiki energy harmonizing is that you are the creator of your perception, your experiences and your life regardless of external circumstance and limiting beliefs. We are all here to discover and serve a purpose, a personal mission to expose the light not only within ourselves, but in those around us.

YOGA, MEDITATION AND SELF-REALIZATION

The practice of yoga is certainly not a new tradition. Hatha yoga has been shown in ancient text to date as far back as 800 years. In what we call the Western world, the first school of Hatha was established in 1918. Yoga is defined as the uniting of the mind, body and spirit, to your higher consciousness, God, Divine, or

Source. It has been noted as a healing science, as regular practice will increase awareness and decrease disease. Yoga is a practice of self-study or self-realization. I like to think of it as a coming home to yourself. Some of the health benefits of practicing yoga and meditation regularly are:

• Decreases anxiety and helps you release from "fight or flight" mode, creating more time spent in a clam state of peace.

• Encourages a cultivation of non-judgement, self-trust, balanced ego, and genuine kindness.

• Increases flexibility, muscle strength, respiration, circulatory health, along with energy and vitality.

Yoga offers eight limbs or basic guidelines on how to live a meaningful or soulful life. The first four aspects lean in a more practical direction and are designed to prepare you for the second half of the journey, the pathway to Samadhi, described as a pure state of ecstasy. The last four aspects relate to meditation and creating a space for you to hear the whispers of your soul. This part of the journey requires that you fully embody your authenticity.

1. Yamas - which follow the golden rule of "treat others as you wish to be treated," drawing focus on your own behavior, nonviolence, truthfulness, non-stealing and non-possessiveness, refining your personality.

2. Niyamas - which deal with self-discipline and spiritual practices, purity, contentment, self-study and surrender to your God, Divine or Source.

3. Asana - which relates to the physical practice of postures, developing a relationship with your body and energetic awareness of yourself. The practice of moving the body seamlessly with the breath, learning self-discipline, compassion and acceptance as you meet the body where it is, concentration, and being present which will be useful in meditation.

4. Pranayama - gaining mastery and full awareness of your breath, this is the life force within. The breath is the largest healing system in the body and possibly the one that we take for granted the most. In my experience it isn't unlikely for a Doctor, Psychologist, or Psychiatrist to suggest that you take deep breaths to calm yourself down. I give Yoga a standing ovation for teaching me how to breath! Breath-work can be practiced as an isolated technique; however, it is integral to the physical practice of yoga posture.

5. Pratyahara - meaning detachment from external distraction or sensory transcendence.

6. Dharana - concentration and focus on stilling the internal distractions of the mind.

7. Dhyana - meditation or contemplation, becoming fully aware without any focus.

8. Samadhi - union of self and connection higher consciousness, to God, Divine, or your Source.

In my opinion, Samadhi is achieved through living authentically and in alignment with your soul's purpose. A blissful experience of being one with the Universe and fully aware of all the abundance that surrounds you. Through consistent, daily practice, patience, self-love and self-acceptance anyone is capable of this experience or enlightenment.

I support clients fully on this journey with seminars, on-site and online class offerings for both yoga and meditation as well as a comprehensive yoga teacher training/self-study program. Listed below are a few of my offerings:

• Yoga Teacher Training Program. This course is approximately 4-6 month in duration and is designed to create a deeper connection to self. Additionally, you will learn everything necessary to deliver yoga privately or in a class setting.

• Mindfully living and loving the journey is a meditation-based course. Discover your innate ability to create harmony in all areas of your life. Learn the benefits of breath, mantra and meditation as you embark upon your journey toward mindfulness.

• Energy empowering and clearing meditations based on the lunar energy. These offerings are reiki inspired and include connecting to higher self, breath-work, chanting, mantra, emotional freedom tapping, fire ceremonies, meditation and yoga nidra.

• Refreshing retreats in Sedona, Arizona. This offering is a mindful journey of the heart! A time for reflection, relaxation and rejuvenation for your spirit. This all-inclusive retreat will invite you to find clarity, purpose, and freedom. A space to fully immerse in your heart's desire. Itinerary includes yoga and meditation, reflection and release activities, day trips to Sedona with Vortex visit, outdoor adventures and personal loving support!

REIKI AND CHAKRA ENERGY SYSTEMS

Reiki energy harmonizing/healing is an amazing gift that was shared with me during an interesting time in my journey. I hold a master level in this modality, which has been a vital skill that serves to guide and support clients in discovering their inner light and purpose successfully. I offer on-site and online seminars, workshops, harmonizing sessions and spiritual attunement sessions that are loaded with information on energy, including:

• Reiki level 1, 2 and 3 Attunement. Attunement is the process of transferring the power of universal life force energy to the student by a reiki master.

• Chakra 101. Exploring energetic anatomy. Clients are provided a complete guide on the chakra system and an open discussion about how chakras impact your life, as well as how to create inner balance and harmony.

Reiki is a "spiritually guided life force energy." This modality takes a holistic approach to harmonizing/healing the body. The technique aids in the reduction of stress and promotes relaxation and healing. It is administered by "laying on hands" and is based on the idea that an unseen "life force energy" flows through us and is what causes us to be alive. If one's "life force energy" is low, then we are more likely to get sick or feel stress, and if it is high, we are more capable of being joyful and healthy. I have thoroughly studied reiki energy along with the chakra energy system for the last decade. A chakra is literally a vortex of energy, connecting our physical existence to higher and deeper non-physical realms. These seven energetic set points in the body act as filters for the experiences that we encounter from past lives all the way to present moment. What we generate determines much of what we receive, hence the idea of karma. A blockage or imbalance in one or several of the chakras can initiate mental, emotional, physical and spiritual ailments. When properly balanced the seven chakras work together to create the optimal life. I personally use reiki, yoga, crystals, sound healing vibration, and mantra mediation to heal and restore chakra balance. I have a daily practice of praying, visualizing, and aligning my mind, body and spirit so that I may present as the very best version of myself. Each one of the seven chakras are responsible for the emotional and physical energy within a certain point of your body. The following is a map of the chakra location and purpose:

1. The root chakra "Muladhara" is located at the base of the base of the spine and manages your security, stability and assurance.

2. The sacral chakra 'Svadhishthana" located above the root, below the belly button manages your emotional resilience, including guilt, shame, and co-dependency, along with being a center for creativity and sexuality.

3. The solar plexus chakra "Manipura" is known as the "fire of desire" just above the belly button. This super powered chakra manages self/ego, confidence, acceptance, and self-belief.

4. The heart chakra "Anahata" is located above the solar plexus in the center of the chest. This amazing space of energy, light, and soul expression manages, love, compassion, forgiveness, and gratitude. I believe the space of the heart chakra is where your voice of purpose lives. Every morning before I get out of bed, I

pause in stillness with both palms on my heart space and listen for the whisper of my soul.

5. The throat chakra "Vishudda" is located in the center of the throat space. This is where we enliven self-expression, courage and authenticity.

6. The third-eye "Ajna" is our connection to clear thinking, imagination, self-reflection, and intuition. It is nestled in the center of the brain near the pineal gland.

7. The crown chakra "Sahasrara" is your spiritual connection to higher consciousness, God, Divine, or Source. A balanced crown chakra allows you to feel freedom, unity, and complete harmony!

Combining the knowledge and practices of yoga, meditation, reiki, and chakra energy allows you to truly know yourself and in this knowing self-love, self-trust, and self- acceptance ignite the light of the soul.

BEGINNING THE JOURNEY

Treat this journey the same as you would a new friendship, get excited about it, prepare for new adventures, surrender to the unknown and have fun! When I was running one morning, I was thinking of ways I could encourage clients to embrace this way of life and this is what I heard:

S.I.M.P.L.E. – Seriously Imagine More Positive Life Experiences!

What is pulling on your heart strings right now? What in your life is screaming for your attention and transformation? Honor everything that you hear and write it down. On the same piece of paper write down your dreams, your wishes and your desired outcome.

Now, let's pick a mantra to help you eliminate distraction. A mantra encourages you to practice activation of free will, no longer ruled by the seeds of your mind. Practicing mantra will reduce the mental fluctuations of your mind quickly. If the mind is steady your body will follow. Allow me to share a few that I have used to embody soulful living:

- "Everything I need is already within me"

- "I am open to receive all that the universe has for me"

- "I can achieve anything I desire"

- "I am present in this moment accepting who I am where I am"

- "I love myself, I trust myself, I am enough"

- "My life is filled with abundance and prosperity"

Is there a mantra that resonates with you here? Maybe something is already entertaining your mind that is perfect for you in this moment. Use your mantra as often as possible to bring yourself back to present moment awareness.

Meditate with your mantra. Meditation is not a practice of sitting in a dark room as still as possible, I tried that for a minute and all I could feel was chest pain. Look for guided meditation, offerings that take you on a journey. I have developed specific meditations for my clients based on their individual needs, I would be honored to do this for you too. You can also find some great offerings on YouTube. Yoga nidra specifically works with mantra meditation.

This practice is referred to as "yogic sleep," how can you go wrong with that!

Make yourself a yoga date and take your mantra with you! Research some local yoga studios or try a few online if that feels better. If you're a beginner find a basic class and remember the guidelines of yoga, this practice is a judgement free zone. In my yoga classes I constantly remind my clients that the mind tells the body and the body responds. I remember my early days on the yoga mat I used the energy of force to get my body to look a certain way, it was my ego's need to look like my mat neighbor who had been practicing yoga forever.

What I have learned is that force is not necessary, everybody is designed different, everybody will look different and feel different, so I started embracing my differences. My yoga still teaches me self-love, compassion and trust. What I learn on my mat I live off my mat. If you start to feel distracted or frustrated inwardly repeat your mantra. I make it a point to try everything twice, just in case I missed something the first time. Success lies in your ability to love and accept yourself exactly where you are!

Finally, schedule yourself a reiki or energy harmonizing session. This is a holistic modality that is purely designed to create inner harmony. I understand the dis-ease that is created by unfortunate life circumstances, anxiety infused lifestyles, hopelessness and the need to be free from limiting beliefs. Allow yourself to experience this amazing energetic tune-up.

Some of us have spent our lifetime living in a state of dis-ease. Open your heart, your mind and your soul to receive the gift of a new life. Allow yourself to transform, to release from cultural conditioning and live fully!

 Create a daily practice of making the choice to live in your truth, your light and your purpose. The universe is here to guide you, love you and support your destiny toward wholehearted living.

My mission is to support awakening soul's in defining and aligning with their mission and purpose. This is an invitation from the universe, mother earth, your God to awaken, the stage has been set, the mind, body, and spirit are designed to unite and deliver the path to your soul's purpose.

Be brave and move wholeheartedly toward what lights you up.

EPISODE 55

MARY GOODEN

Mary Gooden is a fully embodied channel for the Divine Feminine Christ consciousness and Sacred Wellness Advisor. She believes that abundance thrives in your ability to remain aligned and authentic, which is a daily practice. Mary has studied and practiced Yoga, Meditation and Reiki Energy Harmonizing for almost twenty years. By taking an intuitive approach, she focuses on creating a space for clients to anchor their light and embrace Heaven on Earth through an immersive experience online or in Sedona, Arizona.

Mary is the CEO and founder of Divine Destiny Publishing and the host of Shine Your Soul Light Podcast. She supports conscious leaders, coaches, visionaries, and entrepreneurs in becoming published authors by sharing their powerful story, message, and mission on a global platform. She has contributed to ten #1 International Bestselling titles. Her publishing company has created four #1 International Bestselling books titled – *Aligned Leaders, Wholehearted Leaders, Sacred Surrender & Revolutionary Leaders.*

Website: www.marygooden.com

KIM WAGNER

EMBRACING MY SOUL'S MISSION

I remember it like it was yesterday. Standing with my parents in their backyard one afternoon, it was around 5pm when my doctor called. The results of a recent pap smear were inconclusive, and I needed to come back in for another test. My heart started to race, I felt sick in my stomach, and was dizzy with stress. All I could think was "*Not me too. This cannot be real.*"

My father had been diagnosed with colon cancer a few months earlier, and my mother with breast cancer just the week before. The thought of receiving more bad news was too much for me to handle. Thankfully at my follow up appointment the doctor discovered I was pregnant. This was such a relief, the news warmly welcomed as my husband and I had been trying to conceive for over a year.

Within three short years both my parents died - first my dad, then my mum. I was 31-years-old and six months pregnant with my son when my mother died. The entirety of both my children's existence was surrounded by fear, sadness, and loss. Although I know this is not something I had any control over, it still brings me great sadness to know that they experienced these emotions from conception.

Looking back, I really don't understand how I managed to get through those dark times. Losing so much in such a short period, particularly while pregnant, was really intense. As anyone who has lost a loved one to cancer knows, it's a rollercoaster of emotion and the grief is ongoing throughout the illness and eventual death. One thing I remember the most is feeling completely isolated and alone. There was nothing that anyone could do to help me, it was something that could only be done on my own.

Losing my parents so quickly and at such a young age made me think about contributing factors. My father died at age 59 and my mother was 56. There was no family history, dodgy genes, or particularly obvious reason. However, my thinking was that surely cancer (or any other degenerative disease) doesn't just happen.

Rather than being a victim, I was determined to do anything that I could in a preventative manner regarding the health of myself and my family. I've always been a solution-finder and this was another opportunity to look further into things. Once again, I was alone in this journey. Not one other person in my family or tribe questioned anything, which brought back those feelings of isolation. In fact, I was often ridiculed, which made me more determined to continue. The general consensus at that time was that I had been dealt a bunch of dodgy genes and my fate was pretty much sealed. This was how people thought when I growing up - you are dealt with certain things that cannot be changed and one of those things is your genetic make-up.

For me, the most obvious place to start was the food we ate. I started to replace current habits with new, healthy ones. Going back to basics, growing my own produce as much as possible, and cooking from scratch. As more and more research came out, I devoured it. The food and drink we consume, as well as our level of physical activity, plays a massive role in our health.

It certainly was a big learning journey to bring all this change into my life. Every single new thing, no matter how little, that I tried to implement into my family's life was met with resistance. My thoughts and actions were not mainstream, so I encountered a mini battle at every stage. I still vividly remember a conversation with my husband about why we would no longer buy grated cheese (do some research on the anti-caking agents used and how they affect our health) that really set the stage for my journey. It was going to be long and difficult, for sure.

Along the way I realised that some of the people in my life, often long-time friends, were dropping away. Interestingly there was no animosity, we just drifted apart and had nothing in common with each other. It wasn't until a few years later that I understood what had happened. My vibration was rising; when that happens, things and people not in alignment with your new vibration simply drop away. And new things and people who are on your uplifted vibrational level come into your life. It took me a while to realise, but it's an incredible thing to experience. Over the last decade or so, as my vibration has continued on a steep incline, there have been so many changes.

A few years into my journey I joined a Buddhist group. The nun visited a couple of times a year and we enjoyed incredible full weekends of learning. One of our first lessons was on 'Change and Attachment' - this entirely altered my path.

"Everything is temporary; emotions, thoughts, people and their scenery. Do not become attached, just flow with it." - Buddha

---

I was not skilled at dealing with change. I liked things to be how they were supposed to be, all in the right time and place. I guess it was about control - knowing the outcome, or at least thinking that I had some input in controlling it. Our lesson about change made a big impact on my life, even if it did take me some time to fully accept and incorporate it into everyday life.

You see, everything changes. Absolutely nothing is permanent, even if we think it is. As soon as we achieve what we've always dreamt of, or the outcome we believe is 'perfect', the goal posts change, or the ultimate result is no longer the desired outcome. The one constant in life is change. Simply having this awareness made a big shift in my perspective. Although I didn't live and breathe it to start with, I began to look at things differently. From a goal I was working towards, to the fruit that grew and ripened on the tree, to my dining room table – I realised that everything changes every second of every day. Nothing stays the same.

Attachment was another big one for me to learn about. As humans, we are conditioned to be attached to the outcome of things, to how people act and treat us, as well as the almost obsessive focus on possessions. The Buddhist nun gave us this example:

"When you buy a new car you should scratch it right away - that way you are not always freaking out about the car being damaged."

This made a lot of sense. I've always been heart-centred and empathetic, which meant I was attached to everything. I took on other people's pain and problems, got involved in things that did not serve me, and suffered an awful lot. While the lesson on attachment took some time to introduce into my life, it has become easier. Now I'm at the point where I am detached to pretty much anything that comes my way. This does not mean that I don't care but that I am not attached to the result. This subtle shift will change your life.

Nowadays I can witness or be involved with issues and situations with no attachment; it is so freeing. This allows me to help myself, family, and clients so much more effectively. The only area I still get attached to is my family and, in particular, my children. It's a work in progress but I will say that, although I am still attached to outcomes with them, my focus is not clouded and I am able to be responsive rather than reactive.

Around this time, I began to study and learn Reiki. During the very first attunement, I received a message: *"You're already a master healer."* Looking back this was quite evident. From the very first practice sessions I just knew what to do and could feel how powerful my healing gift was. Although I continued to study and became a Reiki Master, the knowledge and ability was already within me. It just had to be unlocked and released into the universe.

I now know that nothing happens by chance. On one of the Buddhist learning weekends, I was given *The Biology of Belief* by Dr Bruce Lipton to read. This is why the universe sent me to this group. This was the key to what I had been looking for.

"I am the master of my genes, not the victim of them." - Dr Bruce Lipton

---

Reading his book sent my research in a new direction. I learned that our thoughts and perception can alter everything - in particular the expression of our genes. In fact, only 3-5% of illness is purely down to genetics. By altering our perception, we are able to alter everything. Our belief system, our gene expression, in fact the entire chemistry of our body are all one. The mind/body connection is real, and more important than I'd ever imagined.

A sense of urgency grew from deep within me. A need to learn as much as possible and I knew instinctively that there was no time to slow down. I began to study a brilliant course through the Institute of Integrative Nutrition which exposed me to the many different areas that affect our overall health. Not just the food we eat, but also our environment, relationships, and so much more. My biggest takeaway was that just as each of us are different, so are our needs. We are all individuals which means that our health is not a copy-and-paste situation, it must be tailored to each of us depending on our unique requirements.

I continued to study a range of different complementary modalities. As my toolbox grew, I could feel that I was on the right path, so I decided to start my own business. The results I was getting were amazing and people were really excited about how I was helping them. Another interesting aspect was that I found a kind of inner peace when working with clients. To be an effective healer, I need to be in a calm, meditative state which brings perfect healing energy to myself in every single session. Not only was I providing healing to my clients, but I was also healing myself at the same time.

While I had learned so much and was able to help my clients and myself to a certain level, I was still looking for something more. Almost like a search for the Holy Grail, it was in my heart every single day as I constantly tried to find a way to complete the healing journey for my family, especially my son.

My mother died when I was six months pregnant with my son. Although I knew there was nothing I could do about the emotions that I experienced, I was concerned for my unborn baby. A discussion with my obstetrician resulted in being told that the baby was fine, there was nothing to worry about. Unfortunately, my instincts were right. Although my son was born perfectly healthy physically, he had some emotional issues that I was ill-equipped to deal with. The little guy seemed to always be in such emotional pain. It tore me apart and I did all that I could to help him.

When my son was nine years old, I watched an interview with Dr Bruce Lipton about subconscious belief systems. He explained that everything we see, hear, and experience from in the womb to around seven years old is downloaded to become our blueprint. In fact, it's also generational, so anything your parents, their parents and so on believed and experienced is also carried through to you. This sets our subconscious belief system which is responsible for 95% of our brain's processing power.

This knowledge led me to think about my son. Perhaps this was the answer to why he suffered so much? It certainly gave me a little insight to his subconscious blueprint. Could it be that he experienced my suffering while my mother was dying? Is that even possible?

Dr Lipton continued to explain that a modality called PSYCH-K© was a simple, effective, and lasting way to transform subconscious belief systems. I paused the interview and found the next available training session in Sydney. During the initial course, my instructor literally talked about my situation - if a pregnant woman goes through a tragedy, the unborn child experiences it **in the first person**. This meant that my son experienced the loss of his mother before even being born. My mind was blown, but I was also so overjoyed to find the explanation that I'd been searching for. And better yet, I'd also found the solution.

After returning from the two-day course, I worked with my son and saw him change before my eyes as he was released from the shackles of his subconscious blueprint. The pain was gone; from that moment, he was happier and started to flourish. What I'd agonised over for so many years was healed in minutes. With the click of my fingers, my son was set free. And he's never looked back.

This was it. This was what I'd been searching for. I'd discovered my soul mission.

My "reason for being" is to help as many people as possible live a life full of love with no apologies and absolutely no boundaries. To replace any negative and limiting belief systems that are holding them back with beliefs that are empowering, uplifting, and filled with love. To heal generational trauma and allow them to be unaffected by societal norms and make their own rules. Wow, what an incredible mission!

Once we have removed and replaced our limiting and negative belief systems, we are free to step out of the shadow and be ourselves. No more playing small and doing what we are "supposed" to do. It's time to say "Yes" to what we want, and "No" to what we don't want. When we do this, more opportunities come our way and we are free to grab them with both hands. There are absolutely no limits to what we can be and do. There is also the opportunity to really tap into our genius zone and discover our own soul mission.

After all my learning and growing, I've come to the conclusion that the answer to everything is love. Yes, pure simple love.

When working with clients I always start on foundational beliefs such as self-love, self-worth, and self-acceptance as they are the very fabric of our being. Without complete and total love for ourselves, how can we make decisions and live a life that is in alignment with our soul purpose? Until we can honestly love every single thing about ourselves, we are not thriving. Rather, we are surviving.

Once we totally, unconditionally love ourselves, our vibration skyrockets, our heart and our energy expands. We are able to step into our true greatness. It's like an alternative universe where anything is possible, happiness is normal, and we are all connected as one with pure love.

It's fascinating that, when you step out of the shadows and claim what is your right (pure love, happiness, and freedom), the most amazing opportunities come your way. It's like you've said to the Universe *"OK, I'm ready"* and it has answered. We know that what you focus on, you create - so if you are not held back by limiting and negative beliefs of old, then there really is no limit on what you can do or achieve. The most amazing people and opportunities are drawn to us like a magnet. Every day is an adventure.

We are in a unique time of a great awakening across the planet. To be able to share my gifts and help others to expand, rise, and feel this pure love is the most amazing thing. Every single day I am grateful for being where I am right now, and I cannot wait to see what the future holds.

While my journey started with heartache and tragedy, I am now aware it's part of my soul mission and the reason I am here. Without suffering through so much, I would never have started my incredible journey. Although I would give anything for just one day with my parents, I am forever grateful for the lessons I've learned, and for the opportunity to help so many people around the world.

Life is here to be lived fully and unapologetically. It is our duty to fill every single day with as much fun, adventure, and love as possible. My hope and dream is that many, many others are also able to do so. xx

EPISODE 65 & 70

KIM WAGNER

Kim is a PSYCH-K® Facilitator; International Best-Selling Author; Reiki Master; Intuitive Healer; Speaker and Educator.

Using her knowledge and extensive PSYCH-K® training, Kim has become an expert in transforming the perception of stress and replacing any limiting or negative subconscious beliefs. This is the key to living a happy, fulfilled life as we work on strengthening our foundational beliefs that center on self-love, self-worth & self-acceptance.

Kim is currently living in Far North Queensland, Australia with her family. She continues to focus on living a simple, happy life while working with clients around the world.

Website: www.kimwagner.com

BEVERLY ZEIMET

MIND OVER MATTER

IF YOU DON'T MIND – IT DON'T MATTER

"Whatever the mind can conceive and believe, it can achieve" - Napoleon Hill

---

*I*t all began in the summer of 1974. At the age of 24 with three little ones under the age of five, my only identity was by association, deep depression set in, my dreams were shattered, and my only thought was *"How do I get out of here?"*

After hours of yelling and screaming, releasing years of pent-up anger from deep inside, I collapsed with exhaustion. At that moment, a familiar voice I had heard throughout my childhood began to speak. *"Who will take care of your kids if you are not here?"* Reality check #1!

OMG, they're all under the age of 5! That means I have to hang around a long time. Reality check #2! Fine, then let's make a deal. I am here to raise my kids and not in the present environment. The main changes I asked for were to get out of my dead-end marriage and Iowa, to live my dream of travel, get my true identity back, and become financially secure.

The voice says "*OK*".

My thoughts, "*Great. How do I do that?*"

Voice: "*Mind over matter.*"

Me: "*What the heck does that mean?*"

Voice: "*Begin living your life for you and your kids.*"

Me: "*OK, deal. I can do that.*"

And I did.

In 1979, the kids and I moved to Denver, I filed for divorce, was well on my journey of self-discovery, met a man who changed my life and the life of my kids, started a business that went to six figures in five months and, to this day, I travel the world. Dreams do come true when you focus, know your why, ask for it, and never give up.

MY WORLD TODAY

"Mind Over Matter still plays a major role in my life. I will share with you the personal philosophy and belief that still drives me today. The mind is a powerful tool and, when used for the greater good of self and mankind, all things are possible.

That inner voice is within each of us. The questions are:

Are you listening?

What was your wakeup call?

Did you take action?

Without action nothing changes. You are the *Master of your Destiny.* It's your free will to make choices and be responsible for the outcome. Planet Earth is a place of learning through experiences. Some great and some not so great.

The past defines the now and influences the future when fear is allowed to rule the choices made on the journey. Humans are exposed to an endless database of information. The internet and Dr. Google make it simple to discover the world of knowledge available at the push of a button.

Processing the information may be challenging from time to time. That is where the inner voice of the true self is there to guide you. That 'gut' feeling or knowing the right choice for you. The key is to follow that instinct.

This takes us into the world of the unknown, known. Moving information from the higher conscious and subconscious into the conscious. We all have the ability to tap into the knowledge of the universe through the power of the mind. There is Physics and Metaphysics. Physics being the science and metaphysics the intuitive or psychic knowing. My first exposure to understanding the psychic world was in 1982 when I took a course called *Silva Mind Control.* Finally, I had answers for my childhood experiences.

I gained a clearer understanding of what Mind Over Matter truly meant. Who that inner voice was connected to and how I knew what was going to happen before it did. Being picked on and made fun of in school led me down the path of instigating as a way of getting even. Let it be known that no one was ever hurt or put in danger.

I was a master of instigation which, in later years, I believe made me great at sales. I also believe instigating opened the doors to manifesting. Think about it, instigate-persuade-manifest. These are different levels of Mind Power.

Exposure to the spiritual and holistic world through the Chakra System, Emotional Healing and other forms of energy modalities led me to deeper levels of conscious awareness. Life was grand and my dreams became reality.

Moving to Vegas in 1989 opened more doors to the world of metaphysics that took me to the next phase of my journey of self-discovery, a new business adventure and travel. With a world of crystals, essential oils, frequency, and more, life transformed.

I collected rocks from a very early age. My childhood playground gave me exposure to the greatest collection of rocks, gems, and crystals - Google *The Grotto of the Redemption, West Bend, Iowa* and you will see exactly what I mean. I was intrigued by its beauty and spent time with my uncle who cut agates used in creating the build.

In Vegas, I began a deeper soul journey through meditation, connecting with the spirit world and sharpening my psychic skills. I dove further into the world of energy and frequency to gain an even greater understanding of how to use this energy in a highly constructive manner. This led to the creation of courses and classes that are still being taught today.

Meditation and reading are daily practices that continue to elevate my vibrational frequency and keep me in a place of peace and harmony.

I always felt a fascination for pyramids, which are part of Sacred Geometry. In third grade I was given a compass and a protractor; little did I know the drawings I created were visions of Sacred Geometry forms that were revealed to me during my studies of the metaphysical realm.

My childhood connection with the Native American Culture began back in the 60's. While watching the TV show called *The Lone Ranger.* The role of Tonto triggered a memory of a past life when I was an Indian Maiden Warrior. Her name is Punkachita and I began calling myself by that name. She became a very intricate part of my life and still is today.

Living in Denver through the 80's, I attended the Native American Convention where tribes from all over the nation were present. Traditional dance, artwork, stone work, jewelry and the culture of each tribe resonated with me. My appreciation for the *Red Path*, Native American Spiritual Beliefs, grew even stronger. Moving to Vegas, I continued my journey on the *Red Path* and began attending drumming circles and sweat lodges. I now have a retreat program called the *Sacred Wheel* which depicts the ancient Medicine Wheel. It incorporates astrology, the four directions, four seasons, four clans or elements, animal totems, transformation and "as above, so below". This powerful retreat opens into the inner spiritual world of the soul, leading to an inner peace and harmony that elevates one to a higher level of frequency and consciousness.

Travel was in my blood from early childhood. My children were all grown with lives of their own and now it was time for me to journey to the next phase of my dream.

In the late 90's I sold my business to follow my dream of adventure and travel. Teaching, doing energy workshops and psychic healing took me to remarkable places. Changing lives through helping others locate their inner voice, learn how to listen to it and take constructive action. Serving others on their journey has been and still is an intricate part of my life's journey and the rewards are priceless.

After a couple of years living out of a suitcase, flying to different places, I spoke the words *"There has to be a better way to travel."* That familiar voice was there once again. This time the message was *"Get an RV."* I said *"OK."*

I made the call to an RV dealership that was located 12 miles from where I grew up. I spoke with the owner who was coming to Vegas the following week for the RV show. Over lunch, he shared with me the perfect unit to fit my needs. We made the deal. Now to manifest the down payment of $20,000.

Several months went by and no money. I spoke out loud, *"Why isn't the money coming in to pay for this RV?"* Then the voice spoke once again, *"Purchase a one-way ticket to Iowa for mid-April for pickup."* Trusting that the money would be there when it was time, I called the dealership and gave them the pickup date.

Everything I was doing to earn the extra money was not materializing.

Five days before flying out, money started coming in. The night before my flight I had $20,000 dollars in the bank. My message to the Voice was, *"Cutting it a little close aren't you?"* The answer came back, *"You didn't need it until now so what's the difference?"* Lesson learned. Time is only relevant in our three-dimensional world. This was a major lesson in patience, trust and surrender. Money came from unexpected sources. Be open to receiving.

The brand of the RV was *Born Free*. We are all born free. It's our actions and outdated database, along with personal perceptions that create our beliefs and place us in the self-made prison that sabotages our dreams. I believe there are hidden messages all around us. Become aware of the surroundings you exist in and be open to receive the messages.

Driving off the lot, I flashed back to that little five-year-old girl, staring out of the car window with the dream of "someday I am going to own one of these". Tears of joy ran down my face. That someday was now. **Remember:** when the timing is in alignment, dreams become reality. Time really is irrelevant. All we have is *Now*. The past is over and the future only shows up one day at a time - and then it is known as the *now*!

When we move past time and allow for events to flow in unison, all things are made to manifest when the elements align. If you allow fear or doubt to enter into what you are manifesting, alignment is interrupted and the outcome is impacted. It is key to have faith and trust in the self and the outcome you desire.

Your inner thoughts, beliefs and actions impact your outcome. This is the law of coherency, the law of attraction and the law of manifestation. Trust in the self, believe in the self and have faith that the energies align to bring the outcome you seek. No matter what it may be. No matter how long it takes. Live in the *Now*.

I shared these pivotal moments in my life because it has led me to where I am today and the work that I continue to carry on. True identity in my eyes leads to fulfilling one's purpose. The journey is always advancing in self-awareness, self-awakening, and self-enlightenment.

VIRTUAL REALITY VS EARTH REALITY – WHICH IS THE REAL REALITY?

Living in the world of transformation, inter-dimensional travel, psychic awareness, astral travel, shape shifting and mind travel through deep levels of meditation gives a different meaning to reality. That which is real to one may not be real to another. That which is truth for one may not be truth for another. One's story is one's reality. If you're not enjoying the reality you're spending time in, change the story.

Reality first begins in the mind. It's the combination of your thoughts along with the collective data stored in the frontal cortex of the brain. Your senses trigger feeling responses that add to the story which becomes your belief. The story imprints to your cells, and you respond accordingly. Your thoughts become actions that result in creating the matter world you exist in.

What you focus on is what you create. If you put your energy in fear, you attract events that place you into fear. If you focus on getting sick, the energies will align and you get sick. Changes are happening at work. People are being fired. If you focus on the fear of getting fired, this moves into how you will pay your bills, you will lose your house; thought takes you into the abyss. If you place your thoughts on being promoted, having more responsibility and an increase in pay, that becomes your reality. Where you place your attention is where energy flows. You design your reality.

Are your dreams real or imaginary? Are the voices you hear real or a figment of your imagination? The brain's perception of what is real is interpreted by one's senses - see, smell, feel, hear and taste. Science has done studies in the virtual reality space proving the mind has power over how the brain interprets sensory stimulation.

Virtual Reality from *my perspective* is a tool for advancement and awakening. Learning and retention has been proven through science to increase upwards of 70% or more. Dr. Google has a library of research to verify the significance of the impact virtual reality has on the mind, the psyche, and the physical vessel.

Working in the world of virtual reality for the past several years has opened a new world of possibilities. Cutting edge technology is changing the way business and education is being presented in today's world. As reality would have it, there are always two sides of the coin. You have Free Will in the duality world. Your choice becomes your truth.

Science has proven the unknown and places it in the known. Metaphysics is the mind's way of energetically recognizing intuitively as being real that which the brain does not perceive as matter and, therefore, denies it as being real.

The Mental Health Institutions have been using virtual reality for decades to help patients overcome fear, anxiety, PTSD, phobias, trauma, and other ailments that have impacted their lives to escape from what is known as the "real world".

What is an altered state? It is different levels of consciousness achieved during dream time, hypnosis, daydreaming, zoning out, meditation, under the influence of alcohol or drugs, or being in deep thought. When a person moves into the virtual reality space it automatically changes their level of consciousness.

The person feels they are in a safe environment, can interact socially, and feel connected; the brain says the avatar they are interacting with is a real person in real time and they feel no threat.

From *my personal experience*, virtual reality is like going into a meditation. The scene you step into opens the subconscious, stimulates the autonomic nervous system, and the body responds accordingly. The brain does not distinguish what is real and what is pretend. What you feed the brain becomes its reality in the moment.

Pretend you are doing an open eye meditation and you immerse yourself into the virtual reality scene where the avatar that represents you is walking in nature. You come to a place in a plush green meadow with a stream flowing ever so peacefully. You hear the birds chirping, the water flowing and feel the warmth of the sun shining upon you.

Your body responds by becoming relaxed, feel good hormones move through your cells, you become oblivious to your physical surroundings, and you drift deeper into the unconscious state. Now focus on the purpose of your meditation at this time.

Why does this happen almost instantaneously in virtual reality? Because there is no static interference. Once the brain's pathways are open to receiving change begins to happen.

Imagine teaching meditation classes in virtual reality or having spiritual retreats. You now have a global reach. This opens opportunities for those who are not able to travel for various reasons.

What if you could take a group of people who are bedridden, or in wheelchairs, on a nature walk? Imagine the life changing experience they would have. Their brain responses trigger the neurological system to fire in the physical body as if they were physically in motion. The cells still have the old program and memory of how to perform.

What if this form of stimulation could help someone walk again? Possibilities are endless when the mind power is released. It is *my personal belief* that virtual reality will change the world for the greater good of humanity, the environment and bring peace and harmony to what we call reality.

The experiences and stories I shared in this chapter are my truth and my identity.

Disclaimer: I am making *No Claims,* these are my observations, my thoughts and experiences. It is your responsibility to do the research and come to what is truth for you.

I live in a space where all things are possible. I create my destiny and my legacy. Who is creating yours?

My vision and mission is to open the door to the unknown and make it become the known. To bring to life "Mind Over Matter" and bring it to a whole new level. Napoleon Hill said it all, *"Whatever the mind can conceive and believe, it can achieve"*

Science is there for those who want to research. Check out Dr. Joe Dispenza, Tesla, Bruce Lipton, and have fun with Dr. Google.

If you would like to go on a journey with me into virtual reality, please reach out. I can be found on social media.

My website for Virtual Reality: https://megaverus.info/1009.html
Meet and Greet link: https://calendly.com/bzresults/30min
Finding the perfect Virtual Reality Stage:
https://calendly.com/bzresults/360-media-events-virtual-stages

EPISODE 73

BEVERLY ZEIMET

Beverly Zeimet is the CEO and Founder of Alternative Solutions With Results, a #1 International Best-Selling Author and Speaker, Energy Healer, and Retreat Facilitator. She specializes in emotional clearing on the soul, cellular, spiritual, mental, and physical levels.

Beverly was born in November 1949. She is the second oldest of 11children. A little farm girl from Iowa with a vision to change the world. She leads with a spark of independence and drive. An entrepreneur at heart and the little rebel who lives within her continues to take her on adventures into the unknown as life continues to evolve. She shares these parts of her journey to inspire the reader to never give up on the dream. It's never to late.

Beverly is the mother of 3, grandmother of 5 and great grandmother of 4.

Her vision, mission and passion is creating space to live in harmony.

Meet and Greet: https://calendly.com/bzresults/30min

SUZANNE THOMPSON

LOVE IS BRIGHTEST IN THE DARK

"The cave you fear to enter holds the treasure you seek." - Joseph Campbell

---

ho am I?

What am I?

What am I grateful for?

Who am I grateful for?

These are the questions I ask myself every morning when I wake up. These are the questions that ripple through me as I go about my day.

When I began this practice of self-inquiry in 2017, it was not easy. And the joy of existing as a spiritual being in a human experience still challenges me today.

Back then, I meditated only when I found myself in crisis, then continued on with my life journey, not yet aware of the pattern of repeat cycle I was in.

To sit here and speak from the heart, as I share my journey with you, is very challenging. I know I am a storyteller, so I thought this would be easy, that it would flow and feel natural. But, my head, my ego, has kicked in, saying, *Admit to yourself that you failed!* However, honoring one of my teachers, Cathy Domoney, brings this light to me: failures are rich learning experiences!

It comes down to two choices. I can get stuck within the failure, which is the human thing to do and is sometimes okay, but I have been doing that for years. Or, I can catch myself on the way to that place and welcome the opportunity to reflect, to remember where I was, and see where I am today.

I have asked myself how I can share my purpose and my story with whoever reads this, and accept that it may or may not resonate. Ultimately, this is okay, I cannot be all things for all people.

"We repeat what we don't repair." - Christine Langley-Obaugh

Asking myself these four questions every morning when I wake up is an honouring of my teachers - *Louise Hay, Deepak Chopra, davidji, Leonie Feast-Jones and Dr Wayne Dyer* – who have assisted me on the journey to stop my crisis mindset and patterning.

That day in 2017 was a poignant day in my life. It was the moment that I finally was told by the Universe, (more like a sledgehammer than a 'telling'), that I had to look after myself first, put myself first, and to make sure that this would flow through to the *"squids"* (my children). I hit the lowest of all lows. When my marriage ended, I was floored by the feeling that the squids needed both parents present. Catastrophising, I felt hopeless and overwhelmed to the point where I simply didn't trust!

My self-faith and belief were subtle hints and, as I speak this now, it's in reflection of, *"What was? What is? Would I do it differently?"* As traumatic as it was, that's exactly what I needed. So, rather than the quick fix, it was time to put me first through the practices of self-love and self-care.

Self-care is putting you first; it dissolves the word selfish. Remembering this is what began my journey of understanding the rippling power of self-love and self-care, and becoming an advocate for it. Yes, I remembered my purpose!

Still to this day, in my own humanness, I sometimes forget - and that's okay. I honour and respect me and it; I always remember that dancing with your shadow, your dark side - whatever you want to call it - is all part of the fun, pain, and emotion needed to be felt in that moment. It's part of the immersion while still being in that moment, it always was, always will be.

I realised that, over the years, I'd gathered so much in the way of knowledge, learnings, and teachings. The magpie that I am (in Australian First Nation stories, they brought the first light to the dark, cold world and will collect anything shiny and bright), I collect all these bright things, knowing they will serve a purpose in my journey, but was never really open as to when they would serve.

"You have all that you need before you know that you need it." - Kathryn Colleen PhD

 Honouring when in conversation with my mentor Kathryn, this amazing aha moment!

"I have all that I need!"

And I've had it all along. In that moment of recognition, my life flipped into "purpose" and "service", and leading and speaking from the heart.

Gathering and knowing that eventually I would need it, I am now here speaking from the heart to you, asking what is my purpose?

So, what did I do? On that day in 2017, I asked God for someone to show me the door! And there, while listening to *Louise Hay* on *Hay House Radio*, was the voice I needed to hear. *davidji's* voice resonated for me at that time, in that moment. That's what a teacher is, someone who shows you the door. You have to have the power to take the action, to open the door and then leap with trust. For the first time in a very long time, I realised that I did not need to ask anyone for permission, that it's okay for me to stop and then dive into the practice of self-inquiry.

Sitting with myself in my own crap, witnessing it, and sometimes being scared to actually share it, gave me the best insight into myself, along with trying my best to be a "present" parent of the squids - that's all I ever wanted. All I desired was to be picked up, hugged, and feel that inside. To hear and feel that it's all going to be okay. But that fairy tale didn't happen without hard work.

This is how the door opened and introduced me to so much, so many teachers, different ways to practice, understanding that whatever works for me is the most important thing. Maybe it was my previous crisis mentality that meant I kept trying something different, thinking it was going to get better? Don't get me wrong, while I was progressing through this process, I still kept slotting that in. Every time I put myself first, I felt a change, a shift, showing me how to change. I don't know if it was positive or negative, but experiencing the end of a 14-year marriage, and not handling that crisis from a place of groundedness, resulted in the loss of my job and income supply, which resulted in me being unable to pay for the house and support myself and the squids. I had to ask friends for help to get me through that space of homelessness, joblessness, heartlessness, and hopelessness.

Sharing this journey, I see, that it all comes back to practice. Through writing this chapter, I reflect and understand that it has happened before, that I am not the first to experience this. Other people have been through this, yet this is my journey.

How would I do it differently? That's also what it all came to; I kept trying different things but I still kept making mistakes. I made a commitment, and I still kept trying. Just like this chapter is not a mistake, it's a challenge, another test to get me through life and be persistent at showing my true self, and allowing this self to show up!

Giving myself the permission to do what's needed, I wanted to do more, I wanted to be more, and I wanted to share what I've learned. Not only for me, this is about remembering that I have what I need before I need it rings especially true with the squids. I have now gratefully accepted and realised that they are my mirror, I am theirs, and we reflect and project, which is sometimes hard and challenging. So, after finding myself in the lowest of the lows, and honouring that could be any situation for another, I welcomed the internal embrace of now knowing that I am not alone! And I must honour that every day. I wanted to be a master of self-inquiry, so that I could sit every day, be grateful for every breath or stillness practice, and not hold on to what has or has not happened. We can't go into the past and change it, and we can't go into the future and force it. So, I do my best to remain in the here and now, the present, right in this moment. That's all it is.

What does that mean? Sometimes, I don't know. It's really hard to explain.

"Being in love, rather than giving or taking love, is the only thing that provides stability. Being in love means seeing the Beloved all around me." - Ram Dass

---

What it shows me is that I am a human who wanted control, didn't trust flow, who simply didn't trust! Why? Because I never felt comfortable sharing how I truly felt. When I did share how I was feeling, it came from a place of blame or shame, rather than from love. Today, I still experience these moments of not knowing who and what am I, and get stuck on where I was yesterday, five years ago, or 50 years ago. And now I want to share that, in that moment in 2017, what I experienced and went through, catastrophic as it was, was actually one of the best things to happen to me; it enabled me to truly witness *"You repeat what you don't repair."*

I have been gathering all these memories, knowledge, stories, lessons, and teachings over the years, narrowing it all to the one question, *"Why can't we be kind to each other?"* How hard is it to be kind and, if you can't be kind to yourself first, how do you expect to be kind to others? I wasn't being kind to myself, the squids, my family, and friends, and I needed to change. Starting daily mediation was a commitment to me, a disciplined practice of learning to sit, to find another way to be in the now. It's about finding that stillness, and being grounded. This practice has enabled me to see the beauty in what has happened to me and how I have the power to ripple the repair through me, to the squids and others; that is my purpose.

Now, I am grateful to have given birth to the children and I welcome the amazing realisation that, for this journey, for this lifetime, I am the perfect parent for them, and they are they are the perfect children for me. With them, I am repairing my childhood traumas of repeating so many different mistakes. What does that mean? I am not putting them first, I am putting me first. I know how they feel and I see the world in peace. I am healing daily, as each meditation dissolves something, every day. And I am sending, rippling that, across the Universe. Compassion, love, and being that a little more each day - I'm sharing that with the squids.

"Love everyone, serve everyone, remember God, and tell the truth." - Neem Karoli Baba

---

How do you practice that? How can I be that? It is a challenge, the human thing. Being in the emotions is hard, but what is harder is the fact that I have been living the lie that I was not allowed to have negative or bad emotions, I was coerced into being something that I was not, and I allowed that control, that falseness, for over 45 years. The challenge to go into the practice of self-inquiry every day enables me to shine the light on my true purpose - for me to honour who I am, while remembering that all is exactly where it is meant to be, right here and right now.

I am grateful to be a light for so many different authors, teachers, and guides; that's why I wanted to share my story in this collection. To shine the light on the fact that we are all heading to that same amazing space, HOME, and we all have a different way of getting there. I have my way and you have your own journey. You may think you know it, and I thought I did, but it sometimes helps to ask for guidance.

"When the student is ready the teacher will appear. When the student is truly ready... the teacher will disappear." – Lao Tzu

All the words I am saying have been said before; they are coming to me to go through me. I want to honour the many different authors and teachers who have walked with me on this journey: The 14th *Dalai Lama -Tendzin Gyatso, Paulo Coelho, Thich Nhat Hanh, Ram Dass, Louise Hay, Dr. Wayne Dyer, Stephen Jones,* and every connection I have made in this lifetime. As a storyteller, I report what I have read or learned, and then share that. How this is received may resonate with some and it's not going to resonate with others. How can I help and how can I be of service? How do I get through this obstacle of taking the action here and now? How do I show you that repair starts with the self? Take action, be gentle on yourself, by leaning in with heart, firmly with minimal force. At your own pace and with whatever works for your approach.

My highest purpose is that I want all the violence in the world to be dissolved, and this starts with resolving negative self-talk and self-beliefs. How can I do that? Not on my own, co-collaborate, lean in from a place of compassion and honour that there are many ways to practice self love. It starts at the Source, the moment the child is born, with the understanding that you will have your own issues, traumas, and stories as the adult. Welcome children as a reflection and projection of pure joy and love. Or ask yourself what did you enjoy doing as a five-year-old? What were the things you did that brought joy and happiness to you? See, and remember, that we are connected. And I want to remind you that when you are born, you were, and still are a miracle! Creation is the most amazing piece of force, it is alchemy that needs to be honoured and loved.

"You are imperfect, you are wired for struggle but you are worthy of love and belonging. You are enough." – Brené Brown

I am where I am today with gratitude to my parents, as they are the perfect parents for me. I am grateful to be on this journey to learn what it is to be in service, to not always put others first, to serve myself first, and that amazingly powerful ripple will be felt. That's how to do it, so keep practicing that. Doing what you say you will do! Showing Up!

So many amazing humans are teachers who want to be able to serve. To bring the knowledge to others to show a way that might work for them. It may not work, and that is okay; I am here to shine the light on the next door to try. Experience the many different ways to meditate, remember stillness, be who you were born to be, and be open to the many different ways to be present. Honour the moment, however painful or grateful. This is what I want to assist people with - to see that there are a myriad of ways to take action, to lean in, and to do it from the heart.

There are many different ways to get there. It takes truth. It takes equality. It takes love. And it takes oneness. All while coming from the place of service. To be able to appreciate your uniqueness and know that you do your best every day to love everyone, while sharing truths. Everyone has a purpose, an inner light, and how you get to see and feel it is to ask yourself, *"Is what I'm doing for myself something that I want done for others?"*

I thank you for taking the time to read these words and, if they resonate with you, I love that and love you. And if they don't, know this - I love you too. My hopes, dreams, and visions for the future are an ecosystem that allows children the opportunity to be themselves without judgement. Knowing they are always enough. One that doesn't require children to filter who or what they are. They can choose to put on the clothes they want, create whatever pictures they want to draw, music they want to sing, whatever they want to do they can, from a place of unconditional love and discovery through wonder.

In the infinity of life where I am,

All is perfect, whole and complete." - Louise Hay

EPISODE 92

SUZANNE THOMPSON

Suzanne Thompson is a storyteller, present parent, founder of a for purpose social enterprise, daughter, sister, friend, connector, architect of light, meditator, activator, imperfect, and practising wisdom in action.

She is grateful to assist, guide and teach children, parents and teachers in every moment, with what they are inheriting: the internal and external problems, while simultaneously co-creating a future with love, BEing safe and filled with hope and joy.

Suzanne lives in Adelaide SA, gratefully with the two squids Jaxon & Saffron.

LinkedIn: www.linkedin.com/in/soularchaeology

PAYMAN LORENZO

FINDING YOUR VOICE & YOUR STORY MATTERS

"*What is the smallest thing you've done that has had the biggest and most profound positive impact in both your life and business so far?*" This is the last question that I ask my guests on my podcast. It also happens to be my favourite question!

For me, the answer, without hesitation, has been starting my podcast. Indeed, when I began this venture in October of 2020, I had no idea that it would be such a life-changing decision.

Fast forward to today, 20 months later, 200 episodes and counting, a whole new world has opened up for me.

It has blessed and changed my life in countless ways, both in terms of personal and business growth.

Personally, it has allowed me to overcome, once and for all, my shyness and fear of public speaking, to become a better listener and speaker, and to be able to connect at a much deeper level with people, both on my podcast and around me. Most importantly, it has allowed me to find my voice.

From a business perspective, it has allowed me to start and build a fulfilling and impactful business where I help good people with beautiful hearts and powerful messages to win. I help these heart driven entrepreneurs get the visibility they need through their podcast. In the process, I connect and work with my exact ideal clients with no marketing and zero ad spend!

It has also allowed me to become a two-time #1 International Best-Selling author by contributing and sharing my story in two multi-authored books this year. And now, it has blessed me with opportunity to invite some of the most inspiring guests from my podcast to share their story in this very book. Talk about life-changing blessings!

I mentioned that my podcast has allowed me to connect with over 200 incredibly inspiring human beings, all enlightened souls, heart-centered entrepreneurs from around the world, in all kinds of industries, niches, and businesses. They all have one thing in common: being heart-centered and all about doing good and impact. In other words, true and authentic *Leaders With A Heart*.

WHAT IS IMPACT?

I have always loved to help, inspire, and empower people. Empowering them to go after their dreams, follow their heart, and realize their full potential.

When I started my podcast almost two years ago, my vision was, still is, and will always be, to showcase entrepreneurs who are building impactful, cause-driven businesses. Businesses with a heart, a purpose, and a mission way bigger than just making money and profits. So that together we can inspire other entrepreneurs to do good through their businesses.

With each guest, my goal is to inspire just one person to do good and, then, for that person to go on and inspire someone else in the process to do good and become their very best version. And for that person to go on and inspire another person. And so on. Because that way, we can create a ripple effect around us, and around the world, that will change the vibration, frequency, and energy of our beautiful planet towards a more positive direction.

Not any single individual can change the world by themselves. However, each and every one of us can make a positive change and have a positive impact around us, in our own circle of influence. No matter how small or insignificant it might seem to us, as every little bit adds up, and does so pretty fast.

In Math, I+I may equal 2 but in real life, in terms of impact, I+I=II, I+I+I=III, I+I+I+I=IIII etc. When two, three or more people come together who are fully aligned around the same goal, values, vision and purpose, their efforts exponentially explode. This is how we can create a ripple effect around us and the world.

That is precisely my goal in terms of what I want to achieve with my podcast. To build a platform that brings together heart-centered entrepreneurs who are building impactful businesses. To showcase them, and their stories, so that we can inspire other entrepreneurs to do good with their businesses. And, in the process, to create a global *Leaders With A Heart* movement that builds and supports businesses with a heart, purpose, and mission.

FIND YOUR VOICE

Let's define what *"finding your voice"* means and explore the two most common obstacles to overcome in order to find your voice. The first obstacle is to overcome whatever mental block we have that prevents us from sharing our story. The second one is that we often do not value our story, gifts, or message enough, and falsely believe that they do not matter. Let's take a look at each of these in detail.

The first challenge to finding your voice: your own mental blocks and false beliefs.

One of the most common reasons that holds people back from starting their podcast and sharing their message is that they feel that their story and voice don't matter.

After each round of my *"3 Week Launch Your Podcast Challenge"*, I ask my students and Alumni what is the # 1 reason holding them back from launching their podcast. The most common answer so far has been,

"Who am I? I don't have 55 PhD's after my name. I don't have a large audience. I'm not a celebrity. I'm not the most eloquent, the most good looking or the most experienced. Why would others to listen to me?"

In light of that, to find your voice, you must get up the courage to open up, put yourself out there, and share your story, gift, and message with the world.

We all go through our fair share of dark times, challenges, heartbreaks and tragedies. These events and phases of our lives are painful. However, they are meant to happen for us to learn, grow, and go to the next level of our evolution both in the physical realm and at the soul level.

Then, those dark times and challenges, become our Story. Our Story becomes our Gift. Finally, our Gift becomes our responsibility and duty to the world.

One of the main realizations I've had in my awakening and through my podcast conversations with over 200 wonderful people during the last 20 months, is that life is a school for us to learn the lessons we need. If all we do is learn those lessons to become a better person, then that is beautiful, but we are only utilizing 10% of the true potential of why we are here. The other 90%, the gold, is taking those gifts and sharing them with the world, so that we can all benefit from them and collectively rise.

We do that through many ways. Some people do it through writing, others through music, singing, and dancing. Others still, through painting, drawing, acting etc. I do it through podcasting. Finding the most comfortable way to express yourself and share your story, is part of the journey to find your voice.

Part of finding your voice is overcoming what's holding you back to share your story. Because we all have a story, no exception. Even a three-year child has a voice. In 99% of the cases, what's holding us back is internal. *"I'm shy, who am I to talk? I'm not an expert. I don't have an audience. I don't have multiple PhD's. I don't express myself effectively. I'm not attractive."* Whatever is holding you back, accept it, and find the courage to go beyond it to share your message.

The most authentic and profound way to share your story, (this is what I use in my own podcast and teach my students), is to never speak from a script, or your mouth, but from your heart. People want to know you, the real authentic you, the person behind the titles.

This is what my podcast is all about. Looking under the hood, so to speak. Seeing what's in your heart and having heart-to-heart conversations to get the know the guests I am talking to as real people, first and foremost as human beings. We are *Leaders With A Heart* because we do business with people we like, trust, and relate to.

When we are looking for a professional, be it a realtor, lawyer, coach, baker, or mechanic, we make sure they are qualified with all relevant credentials. But the one we select and do business with is the person we connect with the most as a human being. If we can't connect with them as a person, it doesn't matter how many PhD's they have or how long they have been in business.

YOUR STORY MATTERS

The second obstacle is that we do not value our strengths, skills, and story for what they truly are - because they are second nature to us, so they appear as nothing worthwhile, and we take them for granted. It takes someone else with a fresh set of eyes to see our story as not only valuable, but gold.

I have lost track of how many times, even after speaking with someone for just a few minutes, I tell them *"Wow that's a powerful story!"* Or *"This needs to be shared."* Or *"This is where your true gift is."* While they thought that their story was not important or, worse, that they didn't have a story to begin with!

Whatever you went through, and only God knows all that you, and I, and we, have been through - it was all for a reason. Not to punish you but to assist you in growth and evolution, on physical and soul levels. We all came here for a specific reason - to experience things, learn from them, share our gifts accumulated through our experiences, and share our story with others so that we can all benefit and collectively rise.

As mentioned earlier, even if your story can inspire just one person and then that person goes on to inspire just one person, and another, and then that person inspires someone else, and so on, before long it will have created an unstoppable ripple effect. Not just around you but one that will spread around the world. This is what we can all do, in our own small and unique ways, to create positive change, to have a positive impact, and contribute to making the world a better place. One person at a time. One impact at a time.

Another beautiful aspect of sharing our stories is that we can learn from each other at all times and in the least expected ways and moments.

My podcast has been instrumental in my ongoing education through having these wonderful conversations, not only with enlightened entrepreneurs but also with people who are true experts in their respective fields. Talking with international experts across all fields and industries has taught me so much, not only about things and topics I thought I knew about, but, most importantly, about issues and concepts I had no idea even existed!

It doesn't matter if you are the interviewer or the interviewee, you're always learning. You might hear something that will make you think "*Oh wow, I hadn't thought about it that way*", or you might hear something in a different way that may resonate with you deeply in that very moment. Something that you might have heard countless times before but the way you heard or when you heard it, in that moment, it was right for you to hear it; it makes so much sense and clicks at the deepest level.

I've experienced this countless times, on a daily basis, not only when I'm interviewing others but later on, when I'm listening to those conversations. That is the beauty of sharing our experiences and our insights with others. It might very well help us understand a powerful principle that we might have otherwise missed.

By sharing your story and your gifts with others, it may also make you understand and realize their full power. And that's where the real magic is, where the real growth occurs. For all. For the person you're talking to, the person who is listening to it, and for you as well.

In that process of mutual sharing, we begin to realize and understand why what we have been going through in our life occurred. The reasons behind them, what they were trying to teach us, and what lessons they bring to our lives.

This will lead us to understand that our story, even though we might feel that it is meaningless, does matter. That we all have a story worth telling and worth sharing.

Finding your voice is about understanding what's holding you back, accepting it, going beyond it, and then sharing it with the world in an authentic way. In a way that is not from a script but from the heart. This is where your Story, your Gift will fulfill its true and full potential.

Even if your story can inspire, empower, and help just ONE person, then that is a success. It is worth sharing.

Share your story through whatever means is most comfortable, convenient, and natural for you. For me, it's through podcasting and now, publishing. For you, it might be through writing, music, singing, dancing, painting, drawing, or poetry. Whatever way you can express yourself authentically from the heart to share your gift with the world, do it. This is what finding your voice is all about.

Having a story worth sharing doesn't mean that you must have beaten a world record, or done a million dollar launch in 24 hours, or solo-crossed the Atlantic in a boat. While those would be truly incredible stories, for you and me, the good news is that our story doesn't need to be that outlandish.

As mentioned earlier, where you are now is the result of overcoming all the obstacles, challenges, dark times, heartbreaks, and tragedies, as well as the successes and triumphs you have achieved. These are definitely worth sharing and telling. You'll find that others will be not only glad but grateful that you have taken the time to open up authentically to share your story. Your story will be someone else's light and guide.

My goal, objective, and the ultimate reason behind my podcast has been to showcase these heart- centered people's inspiring, empowering, powerful, and impactful stories. So that, together, we can inspire others to also do good through their businesses. As well as making my guests and audience understand and realize that their story does matter. That their voice does matter. And to help them overcome the mental blocks of *"I'm just a normal person, I have an ordinary life, what do I have to tell? Who am I to speak and who is going to listen to me?"* in order for them to open their hearts and share their gifts through their story.

The greatest feeling is hearing others say, *"Oh wow what a story, you're so inspiring and courageous! Thank you for sharing your story. This has helped me a lot!"* After hearing that, you start to realize, *"Wow, my story matters!"* and that you do have a lot more stories to share that will inspire, empower, and positively impact others.

Our life story is always with us, we just need to see it for what it truly is - a beautiful, inspiring, empowering, and impactful gift that is not only for us but to share with the world.

Your story is a wonderful gift to the person who is one, two or three steps behind you, who is going through what you have already experienced. Someone else's story might be a gift and a light for you. It all comes back in circles. We all learn from each other at all times.

Ultimately, your voice does matter. Your story matters. Find what way is the most natural for you to share your story with the world

- and share it. Share it in an authentic way, from the heart. The more authentic, the deeper your story will resonate with your audience.

Remember that, by helping others, we all rise. So let's share our wonderful gifts, (some that may still be laying dormant), with the world so that we can not only help others but also so that we can fully understand their true meaning and potential.

So what is YOUR story? And how are you going to share that with the world?

I'd love to connect with you and invite you to share your powerful story in my podcast in the near future. And who knows, if your story is truly a goosebump-inducing one, you could be invited to share it in a next edition of *Leaders With A Heart* multi-authored books.

EPISODE 100

PAYMAN LORENZO

Payman Lorenzo is a Humanist, an International Impact Driven Entrepreneur, a Connector, Cheerleader, Podcaster and a #1 International Best Selling Author. He is a strong advocate of building impactful businesses.

As the founder and host of the Leaders With A Heart Podcast, Payman showcases heart centered entrepreneurs building impactful businesses in order to inspire other entrepreneurs to do good with their businesses.

He loves helping, connecting and empowering people to go after their dreams and share their transformational stories. Podcasting has changed and blessed his life in many ways, most impactful of all, finding his Voice.

He is on a mission to empower Heart Centered Entrepreneurs launch their Podcast to attract their ideal clients with zero ad spend and find their voice so they can amplify their Impact.

Payman has lived in ten countries on four continents and speaks six languages. He is currently based in Toronto, Canada.

Calendly: https://calendly.com/leaderswithaheart/leaders-with-a-heart

RANDY BROWN

THE INVISIBLE IMPACT CHANGES ALL

As a native Iowan, I'm familiar with agriculture, crops, and corn. Although I grew up in town, not on a farm, it becomes part of who you are in the Midwest. It has always amazed me that the frozen fields of winter become alive in the spring with planting. Each fall the yield is plentiful, making it possible for many people around the globe to eat.

There is an old tale about a farmer who was famous for having a small hole in the pockets of his overalls. He started each day by filling his pockets with corn kernels, then went from field to field, visiting people he didn't know. Once they met him, they knew he was a friend for life. His friendship was sought by many, although he seemed to randomly select those he spent time with. Each fortunate soul was taken with his wise words and warmth as he was a grand listener who wanted to know about the life of each farmer he visited. Every story was different, yet they all had one thing in common - trial, pain, and adversity had taken a toll on every farmer's family.

Over and over, the stories of their misfortune took over the story of their past. The old farmer, who was a marvelous storyteller, captivated those who listened, especially the youngsters. He paid special attention to them knowing that someday soon they would be in the same situation with their own families. Talk of faith, patience, good habits, selflessness, and a positive outlook were the topics of every visit. But it was his very last action that made the biggest impact.

The wise farmer already knew about the misfortunes of the last family he visited and their inability to produce the previous season's crops. Leading each family to their field, he walked slowly, saying nothing. Upon their return to the farm, he bid them farewell and asked them to promise not to plant any crops during the upcoming planting season. Confused and silent, they all nodded their heads with a half-smile. The wise man made his way down the gravel road to return home.

Imagine their surprise when spring brought acres and acres of tiny corn sprouts. Perfectly in line, they were spaced the same number of inches apart and seemed to go forever! The family stared at the tiny sprouts, then stared at each other without a sound. Was it a miracle, or just an exercise in faith? It was up to them to figure that out because they never saw the wise farmer again. That fall, they picked and sold more corn than ever, filling their silos with leftovers. Yet more corn was coming from the fields – by far the largest crops in their history!

You might think that our world is void of people like the wise farmer is in this story. The truth is that our world is overwhelmed with people who are just as influential. It's just that they don't yet know the secret of the story. During their silent walks in the fields, the farmer dropped seeds to the ground through the perfectly sized hole in his pocket. Somehow, there were enough seeds to make an average crop, even in misbelief. But it was those with unbridled faith who witnessed the harvest of massive proportions. So, do you think the world is capable of seed droppers, even given its current status? You better believe the answer is yes, and you are the one the old, wise farmer is counting on!

When I originally heard this story, I took it with a grain of salt. *"Just another story"* is what I thought, although it stuck with me for many years. Every time I saw a kernel of corn, I thought of the farmer. Having personally been through many ups and downs in life, I tied adversity to the idea of the seed dropper. It's taken me into my 60's to realize the story was for me. All I had to do was figure out how!

I believe that part of our duty on earth is to make an impact. The kind of impact that can help many, many people. We are capable of shaping others by our demeanor, speech, smile, kind words, and actions. That's the golden rule, right? But I knew there was much more to this lesson for me. Once I found the secret to the seed dropper, I became entranced with helping those who needed it most. It came up in conversation with a friend, who explained the idea of *"Invisible Impact"*, a concept that sank deep into my soul. It tells us that helping today is awesome, but that through our efforts, we constantly drop seeds of life, lessons, and hope for others to use when needed the most.

To understand the idea of Invisible Impact, think about a time when you were faced with a dilemma, whether insignificant or powerful. You deal with situations and decisions every day and, in the moment of doing what you think is best, you somehow think of a pearl of wisdom that fits your encounter like a velvet glove. Where did that thought come from? Who told you what to say in this situation or how to handle a difficult conundrum. Whether you can remember where that wisdom came from or not isn't important. What is life changing is that you remembered the message. It could have been something your grandfather, or great-grandmother told you as a small child. It could have been a speech you heard, or a sermon on a Sunday morning. You may have read it in the newspaper, seen it on YouTube, or at a bus stop. None of that really is important, but the key piece of advice is. This is the "Invisible Impact".

It's vital for all of us to realize that we have the power of Invisible Impact within us. Since our world's population is closing in on eight billion people, how can we all have a hand in improving the world? You guessed it, *Invisible Impact.*

What if just 10% of us decided to invest into the future of our world? That's 800,000,000 people. Can you image the impact 800 million people could make?

What if 50% of the people joined the cause? That's 4,000,000,000.

If, every second of every day, each of us took responsibility for being mindful of our Invisible Impact, four billion people could easily make profound changes. And it is impossible to even think about what influence could be made if our entire population joined hands. We know it's not likely that everyone would join in on this effort, and it's hard to determine what the percentage would be, but it is our responsibility to decide if we want to make the world a better place. I encourage you to make the same decision. We can only do so much about the future of the planet but, by embracing the Invisible Impact, I know there a major shift is possible.

About five years ago, I became curious about the Invisible Impact concept, and it hasn't left my awareness since. I can recall dozens of times that words from my past have tapped me on the shoulder to say,

"Remember when you heard this very same advice back in 1985? It didn't apply to you then as it does now, and it can be the very thing you need at this moment to solve your current dilemma. It was said so that everyone who heard it would save it and use it accordingly."

I'm sure glad that I was a good listener during my previous years because the silver lining of relationships are the messages that come back to us when it is their time to do so.

The impact comes in many shapes and sizes. I have created a list of several different ways that the message can get out and our words can do their job. In describing how I use the method as the messenger, I also continue to be the best possible listener. When I am keenly aware of the messages I contribute as well as the words I hear, every day becomes a gift for me and the world. This daily awareness motivates me to be my best as a teacher and receiver. If you are one who has adopted the title of lifelong learner, this will heighten your experience every single day on earth.

FAMILY

It is true that we must be careful what we say around our kids. The radar ears of young people cannot be underestimated, yet it's too bad they are skilled fake listeners when something on their iPhone is more important.

Giving advice to your kids is a serious job. Due to what they hear out of the house, we need to represent those positive character qualities that make up a good, well-rounded person. What our family hears at home will go a long way toward who they become and how they behave. It comes in many different packages; the phone, talking to neighbors, language used in difficult conversations, dinner talk, stressed talk, or just everyday conversation. It represents the special opportunity we have to shape the lives of our children through the things we value and how we describe those things.

BASKETBALL PLAYERS

Invisible Impact is a major reason I chose to be a coach. When you look past the wins and losses, there remains a massive opportunity to shape the character of your players and prepare them for an adversity-filled future. I've coached players in elementary school all the way to the NBA; one thing is common to all levels of age, size, and play. They all love to compete and, as a whole, they realize that the lessons they learn on the basketball court will be repeated in life.

Athletics teaches life lessons as well as game skills and strategies. These lessons include the ability to properly handle defeat (adversity), respond to victory in a way to keep ego out of the way, play with injuries, teamwork, comradery, communication, connection, listening, staying healthy, sleep, good nutrition, execution, doing your job, staying within your role, skill refinement, and handling difficult situations in practice and games, to name just a few. In fact, there is nothing like a loss to snap the concentration of a team right back to square one.

Winning is the goal, yet in winning it is easy for individuals and the team to take their eye off the prize. They get a little soft and assume each game will be an easy win. In actuality, they are setting themselves up for a crash. Such is the plight of team sports. Personally, I was aware of teachable moments and made a habit it to mention to younger players that, *"Basketball is life, and life is basketball."* When you add a real-life example or two, it can really drive the point home. Again, this is what Invisible Impact is all about. What we do on the floor is much more than just trying to win or lose. It's all the preparation, practice, effort, and execution that determines the winner.

In my 35 years' experience in coaching basketball over all levels, I can honestly say that winning or income are way down the ladder in terms of my reason for wanting to coach. At the top of that list is to be mindful that each day represents another opportunity to instill life skills into each player's game. It's no wonder so many of our players later became coaches; whether in Little League or high school, a majority of them are drawn back to their sport in some way.

THE GOLDEN RULE

This is such an easy concept, but we can make it very complicated. *"Do unto others as you would have them do unto you."* is a good exercise in many fundamental actions in life including: non-judgment, kindness, selflessness, actions, decision making, and treatment of others.

Adherence to this rule would sure help our world become a better place to live. In terms of Invisible Impact, good deeds and kindness would be witnessed many more times for others to see. Good deeds are powerful examples that remind us about how to properly address and treat people. Every time a young person sees a good act, it reminds them to do the same. It's that simple. What holds us back is disregarding a kind gesture and simply moving on with our day. A return to the Golden Rule by the masses would have a tremendous effect on life.

THE SMALL THINGS ARE THE BIG THINGS

"Please" and *"Thank you"* come to mind when I reflect on how I was raised; these two gestures impact our lives and the lives of others. No, it's not old-fashioned and their power can't be denied.

Holding a store door for a person 10 feet behind you must be commonplace. If they are an elderly person, I will hold the door open for quite some time. These are simple ways of telling another person, a stranger in most cases, that we acknowledge them, value them, and believe that providing a little help to them during the day is something fundamental to life. Ironically, it isn't when people exhibit these acts of kindness that people notice, it's when they don't. Growing up in the 1960s left an indelible mark on me and I'm thankful for it. By remembering each day that small things are noticed by others, you are doing your part to make the world a kinder place.

OUR ENVIRONMENT

Every day we are reminded of the effect we have on our planet. It's in the news and is often a general topic of conversation. The issues our environment faces are not the key, it's what are we going to do about them.

A few years ago, I read *The Slight Edge* which made a profound impact on me. It's based on the idea that successful people are those who consistently do the simple, everyday tasks while others won't. These tasks are easy to do, but it's also easy not to do them. Over time, the idea of consistency has a compound effect upon the diligent person's life. This concept can be applied to fitness, personal habits, time management, and virtually every aspect of life. I've personally adopted it by picking up a piece of refuse as I walk into a store. Walmart parking lots are notorious for being a dumping ground so, as I walk through the lot to the front door, I pick up and dispose of the garbage I see. The task, itself, is easy to do, but it's obviously also easy not to do it. As we witness every day, a high percentage of people are not bothered by a McDonalds sack or a mask on the ground; they will go out of their way to avoid it rather than pick it up. You don't have to be a book reader to pick up garbage when you're at the store, but I feel we do have an obligation to pitch in. It is "our world" and, by taking that stance, you will realize that all garbage on the ground is your garbage - and that's a healthy thing.

The issues around our environment are many and, if we all took this seriously, we could help sustain it over time. In our current state, it's unknown how long it will be until some major components of Earth will begin to wane. Again, if you do your job, others will see that. This might just be the simple thing that puts them into action. Effective, positive role modeling can be repeated every single day.

THE WATER HYACINTH EFFECT

The Water Hyacinth is a beautiful, delicate-looking little plant. A reproductive marvel, it spreads on a pond amazingly fast. In fact, its growth over time is enough to cover a pond in 30 days – what a sight to witness. At Day 15, the growth will only cover a square foot of the ponds surface, on Day 20 its size will be that of a dining room table. Half of the pond will be covered by Day 29 and, 24 hours later, the entire pond will be entirely covered.

Why is this relevant to the concept of Invisible Impact?

When good deeds are done for the right reason, people notice. What starts out as one person picking up garbage or recycling plastic bottles becomes two - it doubles. The next day there are 4, then 8, 16, 32, 64, 128, 256, 512, 1024, 2048, 4096, 8192, 16,384, 32,768, 65,536, 131,072, 262,144, 524,288, and 1,048,576. The simple act of picking up one piece of garbage, if doubled daily, will result in over a million pieces in just 20 days! This is exactly why people should be aware of their surroundings and do the right thing. It will make a difference.

Integrity is often defined as what a person does when no one is watching. Is this true for you? Our thoughts, actions, habits, and character are all wrapped up in what we are really thinking and doing. The Invisible Impact is also wrapped up in integrity because our actions - positive and negative - are replicated. What could we all do for our world and the future of Earth if we simply invested in the Invisible Impact concept?

The farmer gave us a fine example of how to go about each day. Consistency in good acts will equal greatness. A great person, strong family, stellar community, and thriving world are the spoils. And all it takes is a little effort, a kind heart, and a smile! We got this.

EPISODES 136, 142 & 147

RANDY BROWN

Randy Brown is CEO and founder of RBSpeaks. He believes his life is a platform for speaking, writing, and teaching others how to face adversity and thrive to create a better life. Randy dedicated himself to his basketball coaching career for over 30 years including a 20-year stint where he rose to the elite levels of Div. 1 NCAA basketball.

Randy supports men who seek fulfillment, success, passion, and a holistic life in combination with career and family. His powerful story of the tragic loss of his two 4-year-old daughters, addiction, depression, and prison form the foundation for his moving and effective message. He is the author of *Rebound Forward, Rebound from Life's Most Devastating Losses and Stay in the Game*. He has contributed to two International best sellers, *Business, Life, and the Universe, Vol. 4* and *Inspired Living, A Guide to Ignite Joy and Prosperity*.

www.linktr.ee/rbspeaks

DROCELLA MUGOREWERA

I AM NO LONGER A VICTIM; I AM A CREATOR

BRINGING LIGHT TO THE WORLD: AN UNCOVERING

*D*uring your life, you experience moments of joy and sorrow. Sometimes, you feel like your most sorrowful time is the worst hell in the world. I cannot agree more.

My darkest moment was my having to flee from the 1994 genocide against Tutsi in Rwanda when my son was only one-year-old. I walked miles and miles, climbed mountains, and fled to the Democratic Republic of Congo while carrying him on my back. This tragic event not only took people's lives, it left behind many orphans and widows. It created trauma, physical and emotional wounds, a climate of anger, distrust, and revenge, mass incarceration, thousands of refugees, family dislocations, and general social disorder.

Have you ever been in a situation where you felt that your help can come only from God? I felt that way when, after the genocide, it was hard to be trusted. Some people thought that everyone who was in the country before April 1994 was a killer. The ones who fled the country also considered the courageous people who survived, stayed, or returned to the country to rebuild it, as betrayers. There is a saying in Kinyarwanda, *"Kuba hagati nk'ururimi,"* which translates as *"Being in the middle like the tongue."* This is how I felt for years. During that difficult time, however, I had peace of mind because of my innocence. Through prayers and supplications to God, days and years passed. Eventually, I achieved a role rebuilding the country and being one of the leaders during the transition period when we did not have democratically elected institutions; a role for which I am incredibly thankful.

After surviving the horrible genocide that stole almost a million lives, I thought that there would never be another extra painful situation in my life. The second time I experienced not sleeping the whole night was 14 years later, on the evening of June 17, 2008, when I decided to flee my country for safety, without any plan or direction. This unexpected turn occurred after a series of successes in my government role. I had been glad to contribute to the reconciliation process in Rwanda, even though it did not end the way I had expected. I am proud to be remembered as one of the women who, as a member of the transitional parliament and government of Rwanda, championed tree planting to save our soil and rivers, contributed to the ban on plastic shopping bags, and helped to draft a bill that gave women the right to inherit land. I also contributed to drafting the current Rwandan constitution.

One of the debates that took a long time was around presidential terms. *The Women's Parliamentarian Forum,* of which I was a member, convened an international conference to strategize on how women's rights would be integrated into the new constitution, and we won what we wanted.

"You can lose your material possessions and positions, but you can never lose yourself." -Drocella Mugorewera

---

CHILDHOOD AND SCHOOL

Born and reared in Rwanda, with seven sisters and one brother, I was the middle child in a family of nine children. We lived in a house without water and electricity until I finished primary school. We had to finish our homework at school. Some of my classmates did not have shoes. As young kids, we enjoyed going to fetch water for elders, and we were taught to respect them. I remember coming from the water fountain, carrying a water container on my head, and, close to my destination, being stung by a bee. It was so frustrating but my mom's consolation was incredibly uplifting.

I attended the first part of my high school in Rwaza, close to the volcanic area in the northern province, and the second part at the first female agricultural school, *EFA Nyagahanga.* My dad accompanied me to these boarding schools. I went to college in Kyiv in 1985 and graduated from the *University of Life and Environmental Sciences of Ukraine* in 1991. Learning a new language and making many friends from different nationalities, including my better half for life (my husband), were the most memorable experiences of my time in Ukraine. Unfortunately, I lost the album of my classmates. Celebrating *International Women's Day* on March 8 was another highlight of college life; I opened a bottle of champagne for the first time and tasted my first glass.

My family has strong memories from Kyiv. My daughter's first name is Svetlana; she knows a few words of Russian. When we returned home, together with other graduates, we created an association of alumni students from the former Soviet Union (USSR) and a soccer team named *DRUJBA*, meaning "Friendship/Amitié" (in French). I am not sure if it is still active. Because of our strong social connectivity, at one point there was fear of us having a political affiliation. I have made new friends from Ukraine, where I live now and, God willing, we will go back to visit again. I would like to see my roommate, Larisa, if she is still alive, as well as visit my school and downtown Kyiv.

REBUILDING A NEW LIFE AS A REFUGEE AND REINVENTING MYSELF

I am grateful for my parents who instilled faith in me. It has been my faithful #1 superpower companion. I am also incredibly thankful for my siblings and friends who took care of my children when I was forced to be separated from them for almost two years. I did not see my husband for a year. I lost everything I invested in for more than 40 years. My life was in the hands of two strange angel men who could have done anything with me.

God fired the first false angel man who wanted money and gold from me before assisting me to find refuge. He thought that, as a former member of parliament and government, I had tons of money. I was angry, scared, disoriented, frustrated, and trusted only God to save my life. I am grateful that, since 2009, America gave me a second chance to live, serve, create a life of my dreams, and give forward. Contributing to this book is a result of meeting a new friend from Australia who connected me with Payman Lorenzo, a humble and renowned podcast host. Networking and building relationships is my second superpower.

Between mid-June 2008 and March 3, 2009, my daily routine was prayer, shower, and eating. Prayer, shower, and eating. I constantly kept my French bible and rosary with me through this very painful but also joyful journey. I had the best time with my Lord. My daughter was 12 years old when I fled. You can imagine the feelings of not talking to your family for a year and not seeing your children for almost two years. I surrendered them to God, our source and summit. One prayer I asked God was to remove all barriers and knots and facilitate the family reunification; He did it on April 10, 2010. Surrendering things I cannot control to God is one of the best pieces of advice I inherited from my parents, and it works. My mother taught me to be kind so I can meet kindness ahead. She also taught me that something good always comes out of suffering.

One of the things I miss in Rwanda is going to *Kibeho* on pilgrimage. Mother Mary appeared in Rwanda in the 1980s, and predicted the genocide, but leaders did not pay attention to the message that the Mother of God conveyed to the young ladies to whom she appeared. In terms of food, when I arrived in the USA, I missed green bananas, aubergine, and cassava leaves. Later on, I found out that international markets and *Publix* sold the foods I wanted. Now, my friends grow aubergine and rengarenga (red spinach) and share their harvest.

I am shocked to often hear people speaking about leaving in times of "uncertainty." I count all times as times of uncertainty because we do not know what tomorrow will bring. I count every day as my last day and maximize what I can get out of it as well as my impact. I never knew that, after fleeing to the Democratic Republic of Congo in 1994, I would flee again to another country. As leaders, we are called to be proactive and make an impact at any stage in our lives.

What I want the young generation to know is that everyone can achieve their dreams if they continue to nourish their burning desire consistently and invest in themselves. I wish to tell them: *"Do not compare yourself to others—and that is different from having a role model. Having clarity on what you want in your life is particularly important. Write your dreams on a dream board as a living document. Make sure that you understand your relationship with money as well as the limiting beliefs you have. Associate yourself with positive people and protect your body from external toxins (verbal or physical). Read, because good readers become great leaders."*

Sometimes, I am interviewed on my opinion about the *"American Dream"* that says you can achieve anything you want. The *American Dream* is real and tangible. Poverty is not lack of money; it is lack of access to resources. The Holy Bible also says that *"When you ask. you receive."* Are you asking enough for what you want? Keep asking and ask well. Remember that God's timeline may be different from yours and the most important thing is to be patient and persistent. Act on your dreams and goals consistently. Remember that goals not acted on are only dreams.

THE POWER OF FORGIVENESS

I have also been asked where, after all the challenges I have faced, I get the force to keep moving, stay energized, and create. I publicly forgave all the people that contributed, consciously or unconsciously, to my persecution. Negativity is my enemy. The oppression did not happen to me; it did happen for me. I focus more on the good things that came out of it.

"Forgiveness is not a choice; it is a must from God, and it benefits you more than your offender. We have to forgive and pray for our enemies." -Matthew 6, 14-15

LESSONS LEARNED FROM MY INTEGRATION INTO THE USA

"The problem is not starting from the bottom, the problem is staying at the bottom". - Drocella Mugorewera

---

I arrived in the USA without a penny, a friend, or a family member to rely on. I had to start from scratch in a completely new culture. I hoped that, as former parliamentarian and member of government, I had enough skills and experience to find a dream job or do something very meaningful to me. But, I was employed on the 45th day after my arrival, starting with a minimum wage of $6.55 an hour as a Production Sales Associate at *Goodwill Industries*. While I was frustrated, I was also encouraged to become my own rescuer. Before my children arrived, I worked 14 hours a day so I could sustain my family. I submitted more than one hundred job applications, only to be told multiple times that I was overqualified. Then I started to learn English and about my community. I read books, attended seminars and trainings, networked, and invested in myself.

Sometimes, people you assume will support you are the ones who will discourage and pull you down. Remember, your dreams are not theirs. Keep moving and follow your dreams!

My defining moment was when I met my now-friend, Sue Carney, who introduced me to the Network Marketing industry, where I met our business coach and mentor, Rick Gutman. He stretched my mind through financial education. I was shown a way to make residual income when starting with a low level of investment. I discovered that mindset and attitude are everything.

I like this quote from Jim Rhon,

"Formal education will make you a living and self-education will make you a fortune."

By investing in myself, I moved from a minimum wage job to become a business executive, speaker, coach, and author. I am now a creator, and I do not care any more about what other people think about me. I think more about how I can serve humanity by doing things I like, and solving problems. My *why* is bigger than *how* I got where I am.

Why Fear and Harbor Resentment Against Refugees?

I believe that refugees' success leads to stronger and more economically viable communities and nations. Refugees are not a burden; they are a blessing. Refugees bring social, cultural, and economic values to our communities. Our stories are our power! Listen to our stories and you will hear the lessons of resilience, hope, empathy, forgiveness, and love that our world desperately needs to hear.

After noticing that there were a lot of myths, misconceptions, miscommunication, and misunderstanding about refugees and immigrants and their contributions, in November 2015, I decided to apply for the position of Executive Director *of Bridge Refugee Services*, the only refugee resettlement agency in East Tennessee that welcomed me in 2009. I left a job with benefits and accepted a position that did not provide health insurance or retirement plan benefits because I wanted to make an impact. Having a leader with lived experience increased the credibility and reputation of our resettlement agency.

Community education and speaking engagements were followed by monetary contributions and community partnerships. Sharing refugees' stories was at the center of our marketing strategy. Students from the University of Tennessee helped us to develop a branding strategy. Thanks to the board members, staff, volunteers, donors, and all the community partners who supported us, we created a vibrant, financially-sound organization.

I stayed in that position for six-and-a-half years, then left for a bigger cause. I am saddened by the wounds, poverty, trauma, and tension in my community and in the world. As *The Diversity Trust Builder*, I am on a mission to build a movement of strong and diversecommunities where trust, collaboration, abundance, and healing become a lifestyle at local, national, and global levels. I will always advocate for refugees and immigrants.

Coach Ai Nguyen says,

"If we can have generational trauma, we can also have generational wealth."

Your resilience is an acre of diamonds in your inner yard. It is waiting for you to achieve the success and the lifestyle you deserve. You are called to awaken it, water it, and let it flourish and prosper. God gave us wings to fly and flourish!

Sometimes immigrants and refugees are told that they are taking resources from citizens in the host countries that is not true. They give more than what they get. The refugee resettlement program is a humanitarian program. The goal of the program is to assist them in becoming self-sufficient, productive, and contributing members of their new communities. It has been proven that the refugee resettlement program can serve as an economic model for other low income or marginalized communities. I would encourage supporters of a disadvantaged group to check on the program and learn how they can use some know-how from it.

MESSAGE TO REFUGEES AND IMMIGRANTS

1)   Welcome! You are set to succeed no matter the country you are resettled in.

2)   Your success will depend on the people with whom you associate.

3)   Do not let your limiting beliefs - like not speaking the language get in your way.

4)   Do not be discouraged by a few people who are not welcoming. Many are.

MESSAGE TO THE HEADS OF STATES AND GOVERNMENTS

When I was in the government, a few friends prayed for me to leave the government because they were afraid I would lose my integrity. I wanted to stay and attract like-minded people to politics. You are needed and your role is crucial. Remember the reasons why your country adhered to or ratified international conventions, including refugee convention as well as adopted Human Rights laws. It is sad to see the trafficking of refugees in the 21st Century and the denial or delay in assigning asylum status. Remember, we are all aliens. Many have invested in poverty eradication for decades. Coaches can help you find the advanced solutions you are looking for. Hire one and be coachable.

MESSAGE TO FAITH-BASED AND FAITH-INSPIRED ORGANIZATIONS

Your role in the refugee resettlement is remarkable. You can contribute to reducing homelessness, poverty, addiction, and other alarming issues. Wisdom and clarity are needed for better services. Leverage the trust people have in you for greater change and sustainable transformation.

PROLIFE ADVOCATES AND AMBASSADORS

Be glad that you are there. Think about whose life you care about in all aspects. All human lives are sacred. We are all legal citizens of the world by birth. Ask the question, *"What are the tangible deliverables regarding the equity you are undertaking?"*

CASE/SOCIAL WORKERS

Be more resourceful and learn other skills not taught in schools, like mediation, conflict resolution, and motivational interviews. Speaking another language will always add value to your services. Read books related to problems that you face at work.

BUSINESS OWNERS AND EMPLOYERS

Refugees and immigrants have many skills and talents that can benefit your companies. Investing in language access and language learning in the workplace is a worthy long-term investment. Give incentives to employees who speak multiple languages and those willing to learn other languages. Think about other incentives, like daycare, which can attract loyal and hardworking employees.

WELCOMING COMMUNITIES

You are the cornerstone of refugee integration and community development. Learn about your neighbors and ways you can assist them, as well as services that the resettlement agencies offer and the gaps that welcoming communities can fill. Building long-lasting relationships in our communities is no longer a choice but a mandate. Our communities have rich cultures as demonstrated by our food, music, skills, and talents. Initiate activities to celebrate refugees and immigrants during *World Refugee Day* and the *Welcoming Week*. Look for opportunities to celebrate holidays together.

HIGHER LEARNING INSTITUTIONS

The knowledge you provide to future leaders is appreciated and should address pressing community needs. Promote language learning as non-optional. Many languages are spoken in our communities; our communities need professionals who speak those languages in different sectors of development. Also, you can sponsor non-credit certification programs to newcomers. Interns make a difference in refugee life.

VOLUNTEERS

Your work is invaluable. Refugees need a broad range of services, and they depend on reliable and on-call volunteers to help them on a consistent basis. The sooner refugees learn about surrounding resources and get engaged in their communities, the sooner they can integrate. Volunteers help make this happen.

DONORS

Refugee resettlement is funded through public and private donors. For a greater impact, please think about making more donations towards supporting operations and staff to avoid staff burnout and turnover. Encourage professional and career growth and advancement in refugee resettlement. Most donors think about refugees, but they forget about the staff who are not considered as overhead. Staff's willingness to serve refugees is there. The problem is their large caseload of clients who have experienced a lot of traumatic situations and who need more intensive case management.

To learn more about author Drocella Mugorewera, The Diversity Trust Builder, or to schedule a call, please visit https://www.drocella.com Stay also tuned to learn about her upcoming book, *From Exile to Executive: 12 Secrets for Integration in a New Country.*

EPISODE 176

DROCELLA MUGOREWERA

A testament to enduring resilience, Drocella Mugorewera is an international champion for diversity intent on building trust between business and minority communities worldwide. Raised in Rwanda, Africa, Drocella won a scholarship to the University of Life and Environmental Sciences of Ukraine in Kyiv. Returning, she became the Director of Agriculture and eventually a member of Parliament, contributing to significant environmental changes, including a reform finally allowing women to inherit land.

Her safety in jeopardy, Drocella later fled Rwanda alone, bravely beginning life anew in Knoxville, Tennessee. There the unstoppable leader received acclaim as the executive director of Bridge Refugee Services, recognized as one of Knoxville's Difference Makers.

Now a business coach and international speaker, Drocella enhances events with her powerful story of perseverance and optimizing adversity.

Reunited with her family, she continues to thrive, a firm believer in the miracle mindset. The only thing keeping you from living that ideal life you've imagined is you!

Website: **www.drocella.com**

THE BITTER PAST

That powerful voice inside told me, "*You can allow this to stay and make you bitter or you can turn it into love. The choice of bitter will separate you from living a satisfied life. Love, however, will enfold you and give you happiness and freedom. The choice is yours, as always.*"

Angry and despondent, I felt the bile rise up and I talked back to "the voice". "*Well, what the hell do I have to look back on that was happy or free? I don't know when that bastard is going to come up and destroy me. He warned me, 'Nobody tells me no. Just remember that I can wait a long time. When you think I forgot, that's when I'll have my revenge. It'll come when you least expect it.' I've lost my job and don't know how the mortgage will get paid. Places don't respond to my resumes and when I call them, no one calls back. Everything I do seems to turn to crap, and you talk to me about love. Yeah, right! All I've ever known was poverty and people kicking me when I was down. I give my best and barely get a smile back. So, you tell me how this turns to love!*"

All this weighed heavy on my heart as I laid in front of the heat register on the sleeping bags that remained as my bed. I wondered how it would feel to be included and loved, and not have to bear another Christmas full of sadness and yearning. What it must be like to have a family gathering with people who actually cared about me? But no aunts or uncles called, nor did my half-brother. Closeness was not a part of my mother's family. But worse, I didn't know I had fallen for the *Hallmark* and *Kodak* bills of sale. Even if I had known, I doubt my loneliness would have abated. Expectation is a cruel enemy. It's hard to wipe out a habit when you don't know what you don't know.

As always, I expected something huge to eventuate that would turn this darkness into light. Somehow my heart would be released from the nearly unbearable weight it carried. The excruciating pain lay in the question, *"How and when?"*. The blanket of gloom wrapped its sickening self around me. I just wanted to escape.

A NEW WAY AND A NEW DAY

Escape came from my introduction to the New Age groups. Answers didn't come straight away, but through a series of thought-provoking information. Slowly I learned that change had to start from within and not from without. As I progressed, the chains of fear and resentment released their grip. It was so relieving to hear others going through their processes of change. They showed me the power of reclamation through release. I wanted that!

So, very hungry for more, I began to seek answers about the past and even pursued several psychic mediums who provided information and encouragement.

One of them said that the former boss who threatened me was soulless. I knew him as cunning. What would you expect from a former OSS agent?

Another said that my father, who I never knew, had passed on when I was about six-years-old. They said I looked a lot like him. My mother rarely spoke of him and when she did it was never respectfully. My heart ached to know my father.

Mother left her family of 10 when she was 20. Being one of the oldest, she had to do the most work on the farm; looking after her siblings, doing laundry at the creek, and helping her dad out in the field. She was the apple of her dad's eye. It became her goal to get a job and make some money to send back home. Back in her day, that's how it was done. She refused to consider that her oldest sister, Margaret, left home and never sent a penny. But Mother had this sense of family loyalty even if it was to her detriment. She expected the same from me.

The apple of Mother's eye was my half-brother. 12 years older than me, he never brought home anything but trouble and a lack of money. He lived with us when he was down and out, and did so without compunction. Living on welfare, we barely had anything to eat during the last five days of every month. When he was 17, he entered the Navy because school bored him. No matter where he worked (when he did work) he got in trouble with the bosses because he was critical and condemnatory and let it be known that he knew better than they did. He was still in his early twenties when he was extradited to our town after being caught kiting checks and stealing. Mother found people willing to loan her money so she could bail him out. It took her a year to pay back the loans.

All that and so much more. Even then it was beneath him to try to get a menial job that would help put food on the table or pay back his debt. He was one of those people who knew it all. Eventually, he couldn't get a job because his reputation preceded him. His early life was a con, and everything was always someone else's fault. Only once in my life did Mother or I ever get a birthday card or call from him. He said he didn't have the money, but it was easy for him to spend time in bars. I sensed that this was because he could look like a good guy who was super smart. If he knew anyone making a living with a good job, he was their best friend. He felt he could appropriate the things he needed (mostly money), and knew his good looks and winsome smile would always come through. But again, his reputation was fragile, and he lived a good portion of life on the welfare system. When welfare gave out, he did manage to get a job and stayed at it until ill health forced him to leave. I heard from family that he thought I was "stuck up" and felt I was "too good". I worked, bought a small house, and kept my nose to the grindstone. Mother finally confided that I was the smarter of her children and that she was proud of me. Finally.

THE TURN

All the years of my life I felt there must be a God. I left the Catholic church when I was 19 because, in my small town, the church was full of hypocrisy and demands for money. At that time, it was ok to browbeat my mother to give more to the church while the priest lived in a nice house with a housekeeper and limitless food being stuffed into his large, paid for by the church, car. It was ok to not come to give me the Last Rites because he was busy entertaining people on the paid for by the church six-sleeper boat that was parked at the church's summer home.

On a sunny, lovely day I walked into a little country church, hoping to find peace. The Sanctuary was empty, but a gentleman came forward to greet me. I told him I was new, and he immediately invited me to come in and join the others in the fellowship area. We walked into a large room where there were small groups of people chatting, drinking coffee, and having a biscuit. My host led me to a small group that seemed particularly joyful. My host offered that Shirley was the matriarch and the others were her three children and a cousin. They were listening to their mother relate a story that seemed very funny. As he introduced me and explained that I was new, Shirley put out her hand to welcome me; her greeting was so warm and inviting. Graciously, she took me to the coffee service saying how grand it was to welcome me. While she poured coffee, then indicated the accoutrements, I basked in her warmth and inclusiveness. She took me back to her group and introduced her son, two daughters, and cousin, who were pleasantly polite and welcoming, and included me in the subject of their hilarity. Oh my! I had never had such a greeting, anywhere! Shirley asked if I was by myself and, when I said I was, she touched my shoulder and said that I was welcome to sit with her and the family. *"After all,"* she stated, *"it's not nice having to sit by yourself."* I was so surprised I could hardly speak as Shirley took me by the elbow and led me into the church.

All the way home I couldn't help but feel Shirley's love and genuine inclusiveness. It brought me to tears. She was on my mind so much for the rest of that day, and following, that my still small voice suggested I write her a note.

Writing comes easily to me; I had done so much writing in my jobs that it became second nature. I chose a sweet and cheery card from a large selection stored in a box on my desk. I told Shirley how her graciousness, love, and caring really touched my heart, that she was a wonderful light in the world. There ought to be more people like her, I stated.

The next Sunday, Shirley greeted me at the door and asked if she could talk to me privately. She took me to a small conference room and closed the door. She said *"I know this seems a little strange, but I have something to tell you. But first I have to ask, are you good at keeping secrets?"* I indicated that I was. She said, *"I really have to know because you can't share a word of what I'm going to tell you."* I assured her I had kept multitudes of secrets. And so, she began her story.

Her husband was a brute. Always mean spoken, he hated his son and Shirley. Shirley was already in her sixties. As was tradition she had stayed home to care for her family, so she bore the brunt of her husband's caustic nature.

But she said that this week had been particularly bad, and she was worn down. After considering that she was too old and untrained to get a job, she realized getting away to be on her own wasn't possible. The thought of spending any more time in this useless marriage was overwhelming. So, she decided she was going to kill herself. She made her bed, wrote a letter to her children, and then got the gun from the drawer. She sat with it on her bed but suddenly felt an urge to go out and get the mail. As she opened the post box and removed the contents, a small envelope fluttered to the ground. Retrieving it, she didn't recognize the handwriting, nor was the return address familiar. The pretty note inside was intriguing, she said.

I was shocked and horrified to hear that this sweet, loving woman with a grand sense of humor could have ever considered ending her life. As I looked at her, I could see tears forming. She said that the love she felt coming from my words was something she had never experienced from anyone. In disbelief she reread the note several times to make sure it was real. At no time had anyone ever told her that she was a special light in the world. When she said she cried for a long time after that and tore up the letter to her children, a sudden warmth filled my chest. I hugged her and simply remained silent. She said, *"I just want you to know that for as long as I live, I will credit you for saving my life. Thank you!"*

The effect of that day was profound. It has played in my soul hundreds of times that something like writing a note, which seemed so small, so insignificant, could have actually saved a life! My own feelings of loneliness and being different were lifted. It made me aware that we never know what is truly going on with anyone. The fragility of life is significant. The small things we do or say, the unkind things we think, the quick retorts, or the unanswered text, email, or phone call are all remarkable in their own right. We should never take them lightly. They could influence a turn, one way or another.

The Hippocratic Oath says in part, "...*to refrain from causing harm or hurt.*" One day you may utter the words, "*But I didn't know!*" You don't know what you don't know. One way or the other. So be kind.

Be grateful for even the most minute things in life.

It's human to struggle and without that effort, we don't grow.

Be patient with yourself and remember we are all learning.

Serve all others as best you can. We think that life is here to serve us, but we are here to serve life. Once you understand and feel that you'll find freedom.

I love you! I wish you to reach your Higher Self and be at peace.

"You cannot do kindness too soon, for you never know how soon it will be too late." - Ralph Waldo Emerson

---

EPISODES 190, 93, 205, 20 & 210

CATHERINE COOPER

Although the world of Catherine Cooper had been flooded with poverty, abuse and many other challenges, friends, family, and the occasional stranger would seek advice and counseling. Her life was profoundly touched after sending a note of appreciation to a new acquaintance. She was told by the recipient that the note saved her life.

She became a certified motivational speaker and transformational coach, and founded her business, Caye Cooper: Life Strategist. Her great passion is assisting others to realize their genius through finding their personal "North Star".

Catherine particularly enjoys gardening, restoring furniture and scouring antique shops. Her pet parrot, Jay Cooper is often on her shoulder whilst her rescued cat, Catie, appreciates a good snooze on a favorite chair.

Email: cayecooperlife@gmail.com

TUCKER STINE

MY COMEBACK IS MY GREATEST GIVEBACK

*H*ave you ever woken up and thought to yourself that you're living someone else's story? At the age of 40, I had an epiphany, well you could say a midlife awakening of sorts. If I wanted to impact people the way I always imagined and find authentic happiness, I had to do one thing. At that moment, the only thing I had to change was everything.

Just 10 years ago, I was a shell of a person. On paper it was an idyllic existence with a beautiful wife, 2 amazing kids and a roof over our heads. On the inside, a whole different story of anxiety, fear, failure, alcohol, isolation, and hopelessness. To add to that, a 20-year career that had left me unfulfilled, underpaid, unreliable and overwhelmingly under water. There it was, the proverbial rock bottom.

At that point I had remembered asking myself if my time had simply run out. I resigned to the fact that failure was the only option. Until one simple text appeared on my phone. It was from my 10-year-old son. "Daddy, when are you coming back?" Those six words saved my life and helped me reclaim my truth, maybe my pain could actually be my life's purpose.

That was the beginning of one journey that would start a thousand more. To help others find their purpose, share their story, and build human connections and trusted bonds that disrupt social change on a global level. Simply put, we have the power to start movements. These are the stories we were meant to share, not to shame. These are the untold narratives that have always held us back, denying us the freedom to impact others.

This became the very essence of my mission to reinvent my life through heart-centered leadership that's rooted in service, passion, and authenticity. So, four decades into living, I had finally woken up, looked in the mirror and met myself as if it were the first time. This was my pivotal shift into discovering my passion to help leaders, entrepreneurs and conscious-led businesses turn their stories into purpose-driven businesses that are rooted in service to others. I shed the people that were holding me back and surrounded myself with like-minded souls who knew me, all of me. Souls that desired to celebrate my successes as much I wanted to celebrate theirs. My anxiety and depression began to heal. I learned how to set healthy boundaries and ask a million questions that kept me in full alignment with my true values. For the first time in three decades, my mind and body stopped living a life that others expected and reinvented one with me designing my future. All of this paved the way for my desire to focus 100% on heart-centered leadership, in everything I did. It was this business model that granted me access to the greatest endeavors of my professional life. Ones that have taught me some of the most genuine lessons in life that I now pass down to my own kids.

This journey of triumphs and the tragedies has led to what I am pursuing today. Using all of my learning, my investment into emotional intelligence, and rewiring my brain to focus on the gifts, not just the skills.

Here are a few of the heart-centered stories that I want to share with you, each with their own uniqueness, experiences, and teachings that continue to fuel the fire within.

TURNING MOMENTS INTO MOVEMENTS

In 2009, the phone rang and on the other end was a mentor and dear friend of mine, Jack Abbott. He told me about this idea he had of starting a TEDx event here in San Diego and wanted to know if I had any interest in joining the team. At that time, the TED brand was relatively new to me, and I was unsure of what I was getting myself into. His influence has always had a profound impact on me, so my decision was pretty easy. I was in.

It didn't take me long to fall in love with the whole concept, helping thought leaders share ideas worth spreading. Having been behind the cubicle of ad agencies for years, this was a beacon shining a light so bright that I could not turn away from it. For the first time in my entire marketing career, I saw a whole new side of business. Instead of marketing products and services, I could find a new passion in marketing people and ideas that could profoundly change the planet. This became the inspiration for what would later become my dream career, helping people change the world, one story at a time.

For the past 10 years, I did just that. I resigned from a job that had security where I was grossly underpaid, overstressed and had hit a growth ceiling at 30 years of age. Remember when I said everything had to change? This was the first plunge taken to honor that challenge. Following my passion, my zone of genius I like to call it, and my purpose, life and leadership unfolded in front of me, and I finally felt as though my heart had taken over rather than my brain.

Today I have turned that very vision into a fully functioning business where I am blessed to have helped over 200 people find clarity in their purpose, discover an idea that can change the world, and deliver it on a stage that will create immediate impact. Ranging from addiction, to healthcare, education, science, technology, innovation and beyond. Each day brings new insights into the possibilities for enriching humanity. The impact felt is not created in days, weeks, or years. In fact, the impact can be felt in minutes. Simply by sharing these stories, the vulnerable conversations we have and the courage we seek by igniting change. One of my most rewarding aspects of my career is to watch someone who has never spoken in public before, take the stage, deliver the talk of their lives, and walk off the stage whispering to me "I want more of that, this is what I was meant to do."

I find the more I focus on elevating business for changing the greater good, the more opportunities that arrive to grow my own business. Today I can say I have launched several businesses that are all purposely designed to give a stronger voice to those who need it the most. *Voices That Unite* and *Voices of Youth* are helping thought leaders, young and old, to use their voice for social change. And *Voices InCourage* is helping families of loved ones afflicted with addiction find the resources they need to heal on their journey. I call it magnetic leadership and entrepreneurship, when you show up with the right intentions, the right people and the right story, abundance ensues. Whether you're a parent advocating for youth or a doctor paving the way for modern medicine, I have learned that we all possess the power to turn moments into movements, each and every day.

THE POWER OF SECOND CHANCES

There are some experiences that happen in life that come from the unexpected. I call this collateral beauty. This is one of those experiences. In 2017, I was invited to attend the first ever TEDx event inside Donovan Correctional Facility here in San Diego, just over the border from Mexico. Yes, you heard that correctly, a public event inside of a high security prison where the majority of the inmates will never see the outside of those walls again. With extreme trepidation and excitement, I accepted. Little did I know what happened inside those walls would change my world outside the walls forever.

On a cool May morning, I drove down to prison without knowing what to expect. In my mind, I had imagined what you see in the movies where we sit behind the glass walls and watch from afar what was happening on stage. That couldn't have been further from the truth. After handing them my license and going through the three sets of electronic barbed wire gates, I stepped onto the A Yard of Donovan Prison. No glass, nothing between me and the inmates except a few footsteps. A rush came over me like I had never felt, but it wasn't one of fear, rather a state of awe. Within seconds, there I was meeting countless men who had potentially participated in heinous crimes. But at that very moment, they were just people, brothers, looking for a chance to make a positive human connection. I was left stunned, but with a smile from ear to ear that I could not erase. Something spiritual was happening and I could not find the words to describe it.

It wasn't long before I shook the hands of a gentleman who had a clear confidence about him. After an exchange of first names, he reached out in a kind voice and said, "Welcome to our home. If I could tell you one thing about prison life, it's that they strip you of everything and fill you with nothing." I couldn't move. I was left stunned in my shoes, not knowing even how to respond. He could tell I was moved, and he simply replied with, "Thank you for being here today to help fill us up. We've been waiting for you for a long time." Those few words, that one exchange, would alter my life for months and years to come, even today.

I could not get that experience out of my mind. Where most people would say they want out of prison, all I wanted to do was go back in. So, I did just that. Within a few weeks, I reached out to the volunteer coordinator, took my security and orientation training, and received my certification to return to A Yard in a matter of a few days. No one in my family could understand why, but all I thought about was following my heart, rather than my fear.

For the next couple of years, I spent every Tuesday afternoon and early evening inside prison walls working with dozens of men on their rehabilitation courses. Just like I do with my own clients, we spent hours diving into our personal stories, learning about our childhoods and upbringings, finding the common threads we all had and how our fears and failures had determined the trajectory of our lives. These very stories became the foundation for creating more opportunities to develop public speaking skills, respect for one another and tools to foster more connectivity in an inside world where that is often impossible. I co-taught a master class that helped inmates use storytelling to resolve conflict and change prison culture. In a place where leadership is only viewed as the corrections officer, this was one of the first times they had the privilege of becoming leaders themselves.

One of the most exciting experiences was launching the entrepreneurial program with 25 inmates. They were divided into groups of three and each group had to come up with a business idea that they could design, market, and sell to their corrections officers. When I tell you some of the smartest people I've ever met are imprisoned, this is why. Their ideas were amazing, the teamwork was powerful and their desire to impact change where most of them had lost hope was something I will never forget. At one point, one of the gentlemen approached me and told me he is putting together a father's program to help his fellow inmates who have children find stronger ways to make connections with their kids from behind bars. I learned some of the most innovative communication techniques to parent children that I actually used with my own kids.

On a final note, one evening as I was leaving prison, a young man, who is now considered to be the youngest incarcerated in California history, stopped me and asked for a few moments. He looked at me, and with a firm handshake said, "I wish I had known you when I was younger. I think my life would be much different than it is today. But at least today I know that we can believe in the power of second chances."

THE TRUE MEANING OF LEGACY

A year ago, I was contacted by an older man who had been recommended to me for some speaker development and coaching for his TEDx talk. I had no idea what he wanted to speak about, just that he was a kind, generous man who needed some strategic direction. I sent him a zoom invite and within a week we turned on our cameras and speakers and said hello for the first time. I'm not sure what I was expecting, but there he was, Walter Green, 82 with the energy of a 50-year-old. After a few moments and introductions, I asked him a very simple but powerful question. "Walter, if you had three minutes on a global stage, what would you say?" His answer was surprising, but it hit me over the head like a ton of bricks. "Tucker, why do we wait until someone is dead to tell them how much they impacted our lives?"

There was a pause and some silence. I smiled back at him and knew he was onto something bigger than he even realized. On his 50th birthday, he spent a year traveling the country and visiting 44 people who had made a huge impression on him and ultimately impacted his life in ways they most likely never knew. He sat down with each person and told them how much they had meant to him at any given point in his life. The year-long odyssey would turn into a best-selling book. But it didn't end there. He wanted to take the idea one step further during the pandemic and inspire others to share gratitude for the loved ones in their lives while they are still here and alive. This was the birth of his core message, "Say It Now" and what he wanted his talk to be focused on.

After listening to his story and then to my own heart, I asked him another question that would change our relationship forever. I said, "Walter, this is way more than a talk, this is the start of a movement. Why don't we turn this idea into your legacy?" Watching his face light up with curiosity and pride, we shook hands and dedicated our weekly meetings to building a movement anchored in changing the narrative of gratitude by simply asking the world to "Say It Now" before it's too late.

What I did not know or even anticipate was that he would become one of the most incredible forces in my personal and business life by sharing his heart-centered stories with me. Today we have turned his idea into a game-changing movement that is beginning with over 250,000 youth and teachers in our schools. The goal is to reach 1 million expressions of gratitude in one year and exponentially continue that pace for years to come. If you were to tell me that I would be spending hours each week with Walter helping to spread gratitude across the planet through three little words, I would have called you crazy. But that's the power of following your heart's purpose vs. the next shiny object. I have chased those shiny things and rarely do they lead to a pot of gold. I can say this though. It's never too late to reinvent yourself, change direction or orchestrate your legacy when you surround yourself with people who have incredibly big hearts.

And there you have it. A few experiences of how heart-centered leadership found me. For years I had struggled with trying to meet the expectations of others, following a career I thought I had to because it's what I knew best. Settling for things kept me complacent and safe. That was my downward spiral, a journey that would take me to the lowest of lows yet unknowingly brought me to the highest of highs. Finding a purpose-driven, fulfilling life in an otherwise chaotic hell was something I had only imagined in my brightest of days. This is what it means for me to be radically authentic.

Emerson once said,

"To be yourself in a world that is constantly trying to make you something else is the greatest accomplishment."

As I said in the beginning, I realised the only thing I had to change, was everything. By giving myself the permission to be more of me, not someone else, was a pivotal breakthrough. When I look back on those darkest of days, I remind myself of one thing that has ignited the most incredible light of all. I simply say, my comeback is my greatest giveback.

EPISODE 213

TUCKER STINE

Tucker Stine helps conscious leaders turn their personal stories into purpose-driven brands so they can accelerate human impact. He is a brand architect, leadership coach, and public speaker with 25+ years in building personal and professional brands, advising nonprofits and coaching heart-centered speakers, conscious-driven businesses, and thought leaders through impactful storytelling.

Tucker is a mentor and catalyst for generational movements that ignite societal change through the power of voice, including advocating for prison reform and at-risk youth. He has helped 250+ thought leaders take the stage, launch businesses, and share global ideas for change, including the highly sought-after TED platform. His clients have been featured on TED, Goalcast, Upworthy, The Today Show, the Sundance Film Festival, and hundreds of podcasts, resulting in over 100 million views. With one goal, to share a courageous voice and a powerful seat at the global table of conversation, every chance they get.

CEO/Founder @ TUCKER STINE + Brand Architects

619-988-5825

www.tuckerstine.com

ABOUT THE PUBLISHER

DIVINE DESTINY PUBLISHING AND MARY GOODEN

*M*ary Gooden is CEO and founder of Divine Destiny Publishing, a Sacred Wellness Advisor, and host of the podcast Shine Your Soul Light. She believes that abundance thrives in your ability to remain aligned and authentic, which is a daily practice. Mary has studied and practiced Yoga, Meditation and Reiki Energy Harmonizing for almost twenty years. By taking an intuitive approach, she focuses on creating a space for clients to embody Soul-Mastery, a mentorship program that awakens you to your wholehearted mission.

Mary supports conscious visionaries, leaders, coaches and entrepreneurs in becoming published authors by sharing their powerful message, story and mission on a global platform. She has contributed to ten #1 International Bestselling titles, and is currently working on her contribution to a USA Today Bestselling series titled *The Younger Self Letters*. Divine Destiny publishing has created four #1 International Bestselling books the titled – *Aligned*

Leaders, Wholehearted Leaders, Sacred Surrender & Revolutionary Leaders.

As a limitless source of God's Love and Light, she coaches and empowers clients to discover their unique gifts so they may live and serve on purpose. Mary's intention is to restore inner harmony, authenticity, and freedom to as many individuals as possible.

Mary currently shares her time between Sedona, Arizona, and New Orleans, Louisiana, with her husband and loving daughters.

Website: www.marygooden.com
Email: divinereikilove@yahoo.com
Facebook: https://www.facebook.com/mary.s.gooden
Facebook group: Freedom, Ease & Abundance
Instagram: @mjgooden76

IN GRATITUDE

Thank you for purchasing Leaders With A Heart. If you enjoyed reading this book, please leave us a review on Amazon or send it to divinereikilove@yahoo.com

Multi-Author Titles published by Divine Destiny Publishing:

Aligned Leaders – Sage Wisdom from Women Choosing Their Soul's Mission over Societal Expectation with no Regret

Aligned Leaders

Wholehearted Leaders – Heart Centered Coaches and Visionaries Share Their Wisdom and Guidance on Living Authentically

Wholehearted Leaders

Sacred Surrender - Courageous Visionaries Embracing & Leading In Their Divinity

Sacred Surrender

Revolutionary Leaders - Extraordinary Humans Creating Epic Change On Earth

Revolutionary Leaders

Manufactured by Amazon.com.au
Sydney, New South Wales, Australia

11938296R00088